KEY TO SYMBOLS

Science & Technology   Scientists at Work

Earth and Space $\sqrt{x}$ Maths

Human Body   Inventions and Machines

Y ou will find over 2,000 questions on Science and Maths. This is how to use your Flip Quiz: If you are answering questions on your own, just cover the answers with your hand or a piece of card. You may want to write down your answers and count up your scores for each quiz.

If you are doing the quizzes with a partner or in teams, unfold the base and stand the Flip Quiz on a flat surface between you and your partner. Read aloud the questions (but not the answers!) and allow your partner to say the answers or write them down. You may answer each question in turn or answer an entire quiz in turn. Keep you scores on a piece of paper and compare results.

The illustrations are there to help you get the right answers when competing with a partner. For instance, if you are answering Quiz 1 questions, you will be looking at and reading out Quiz 2. However, the illustrations you will see are the clues to help you do Quiz 1. Look at the labels by the illustrations. These tell you which questions they are clues for. The pictures behind the quiz numbers at the top of the page are not such obvious clues, but they may still help you get the right answer.

The questions are divided into six subjects: Science and Technology, Earth and Space, Human Body, Scientists at Work, Maths, Inventions and Machines. You should attempt all questions though.

As you progress through the quizzes you will notice that the questions get harder. Level 1 is the easiest and the hardest is Level 4, but you may find it the other way round. It all depends on what you happen to know.

Levels
There are four levels of question – they get harder as you progress

Question categories
The questions are divided into six subjects (see key above)

Picture clues 1
These visual clues are not always obvious (and they don't have labels)

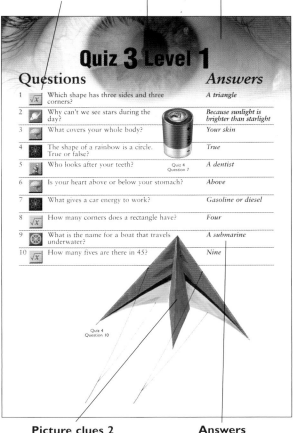

Quiz 3 Level 1

Questions / Answers

		Questions	Answers
1	$\sqrt{x}$	Which shape has three sides and three corners?	A triangle
2		Why can't we see stars during the day?	Because sunlight is brighter than starlight
3		What covers your whole body?	Your skin
4		The shape of a rainbow is a circle. True or false?	True
5		Who looks after your teeth?	A dentist
6		Is your heart above or below your stomach?	Above
7		What gives a car energy to work?	Gasoline or diesel
8	$\sqrt{x}$	How many corners does a rectangle have?	Four
9		What is the name for a boat that travels underwater?	A submarine
10	$\sqrt{x}$	How many fives are there in 45?	Nine

Quiz 4 Question 7

Quiz 4 Question 10

Picture clues 2
These visual clues will often help you get the answer – the label tells you which question they refer to

Answers
When doing the quizzes on your own, cover the answers with your hand or a piece of card

Quiz 1 Level 1

Questions

Answers

1		Which one of the world's most important inventions was first used about 5,500 years ago?	*The wheel*
2		What is the nearest star to Earth?	*The Sun*
3		What do you call a straight line that goes from side to side?	*A horizontal line*
4		What does a mathematician study?	*Numbers*
5		What is the nearest object in space to Earth?	*The Moon*
6		How many sides does an octagon have?	*Eight*
7		What is used to colour cloth?	*Dye*
8		What part of your body do you think with?	*Your brain*
9		When a sound bounces off something like a wall what do you hear?	*An echo*
10		Where do you go for an operation or if you are hurt?	*Hospital*

Quiz 2
Question 5

Quiz 2
Question 7

Quiz 2
Question 1

Quiz 2 Level 1

Questions			Answers
1		What would help you float safely to the ground from an aeroplane?	*A parachute*
2		Could we live on any other planet in our Solar System apart from Earth?	*No*
3	$\sqrt{x}$	What shape is a cereal box?	*A cuboid*
4		What forms over a cut when it is healing?	*A scab*
5		What does the word magnify in magnifying glass mean?	*Make bigger*
6		Which two parts of your body do you brush each day?	*Your hair and teeth*
7		How do you produce a sound from a wind instrument?	*By blowing into it*
8		What must an astronaut wear in space?	*A spacesuit*
9	$\sqrt{x}$	What is half of 48?	*24*
10		What happens to butter when it is heated?	*It melts*

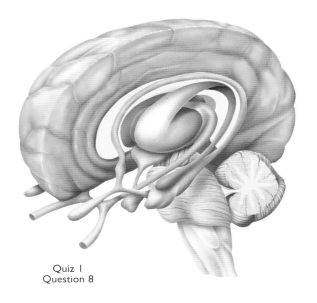

Quiz 1
Question 8

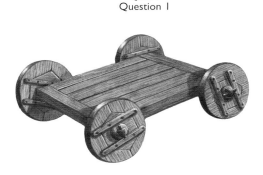

Quiz 1
Question 1

Quiz 3 Level 1

Questions

Answers

1	Which shape has three sides and three corners?	A triangle
2	Why can't we see stars during the day?	Because sunlight is brighter than starlight
3	What covers your whole body?	Your skin
4	The shape of a rainbow is a circle. True or false?	True
5	Who looks after your teeth?	A dentist
6	Is your heart above or below your stomach?	Above
7	What gives a car energy to work?	Petrol or diesel
8	How many corners does a rectangle have?	Four
9	What is the name for a boat that travels underwater?	A submarine
10	How many fives are there in 45?	Nine

Quiz 4
Question 7

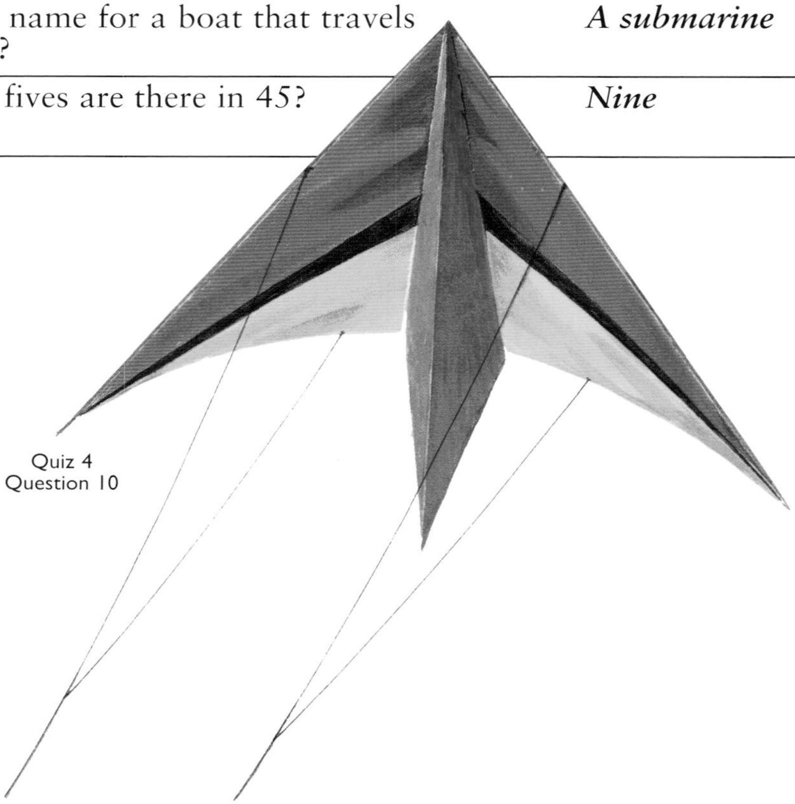

Quiz 4
Question 10

Quiz 4 Level 1

Questions

Answers

		Question	Answer
1		What part of your body do you see with?	*Your eyes*
2		Which do we hear or see first – thunder or lightning?	*Lightning*
3		Which shape has four sides the same length?	*A square*
4		What disease makes you sneeze and your nose run?	*A cold*
5		What is 100 ÷ 10?	*10*
6		What work does a surgeon do?	*Carries out operations*
7		What is put in a torch to give it the power to work?	*A battery*
8		How many hours are there in a day?	*24*
9		What are dairy products made from?	*Milk*
10		Which toy is the oldest flying machine?	*A kite*

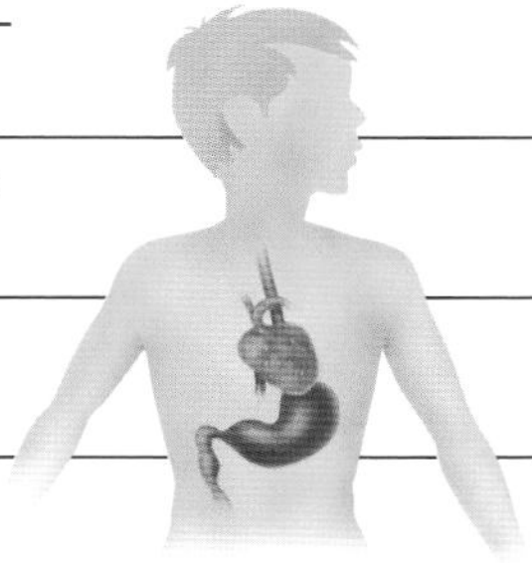

Quiz 3
Question 6

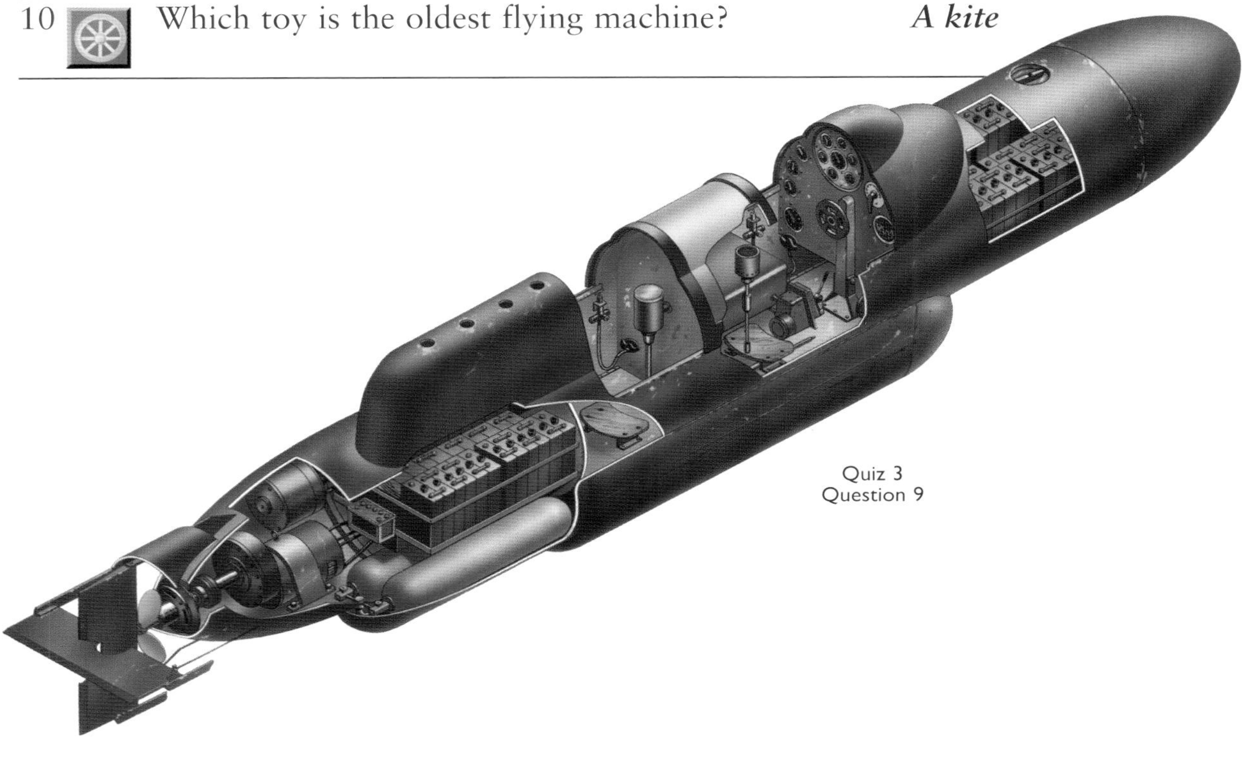

Quiz 3
Question 9

Quiz 5 Level 1

Questions		Answers
1	What shape is a planet?	*A sphere or spheroid*
2	Which tool has a toothed blade for cutting?	*A saw*
3	What nationality was Galileo – English, Greek or Italian?	*Italian*
4	What gives a yacht the power to move?	*Wind*
5	How many centimetres are there in a metre?	*100*
6	What part of your body do you taste with?	*Your tongue*
7	What is 20 x 0?	*0*
8	What is the word 'vet' short for?	*Veterinarian*
9	What usually covers the top of a tall mountain?	*Snow and ice*
10	What do we call the invisible mixture of gases all around us?	*Air*

Quiz 6
Question 10

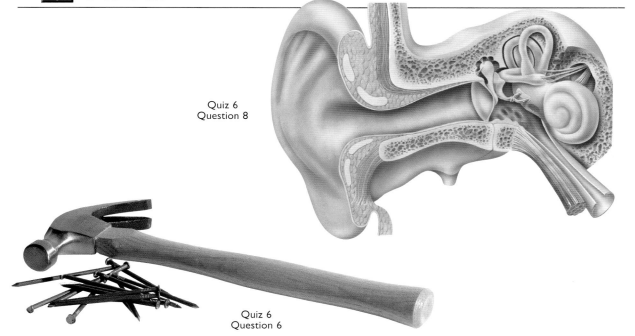

Quiz 6
Question 8

Quiz 6
Question 6

Quiz 6 Level 1

Questions

Answers

		Questions	Answers
1		What is solid water called?	*Ice*
2		Which star gives Earth its heat and light?	*The Sun*
3		Are more people left- or right-handed?	*Right-handed*
4	$\sqrt{x}$	How many minutes until midday if the time is 11:15 a.m.?	*45*
5		Which will float in water: a cork, a nail or a coin?	*A cork*
6		Which tool is used to push in and pull out nails?	*A hammer*
7		What is an island surrounded by?	*Water*
8		What part of your body do you hear with?	*Your ears*
9		What natural material is paper made from?	*Wood*
10	$\sqrt{x}$	Which shape has six square faces?	*A cube*

Quiz 5
Question 1

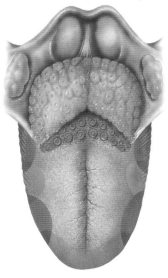

Quiz 5
Question 6

Quiz 5
Question 8

Quiz 7 Level 1

Questions   Answers

#		Question	Answer
1	$\sqrt{x}$	How many legs do 10 ants have?	*60*
2		What do you do to an egg to boil it?	*Cook it in hot water*
3		What are formed when wind blows over the sea?	*Waves*
4		You can feel with your hair. True or false?	*False*
5		What do you see when you look in a mirror?	*A reflection*
6		Is Earth a star or a planet?	*A planet*
7	$\sqrt{x}$	What instrument is used to draw and measure straight lines?	*A ruler*
8	$\sqrt{x}$	Which is shorter, 1 ¾ metres or 150 cm?	*150 cm*
9		Which machine is controlled by a mouse?	*A computer*
10		Do shiny things feel rough or smooth?	*Smooth*

Quiz 8
Question 5

Quiz 8 Level 1

Questions | Answers

#		Question	Answer
1		What is the name for a space traveller?	*Astronaut*
2		What do you get if you double 30?	*60*
3		What is the name of the liquid that pours from a volcano?	*Lava*
4		How many sides does a parallelogram have?	*Four*
5		What has a saddle, pedals and a chain?	*A bicycle*
6		What are the primary colours?	*Red, yellow and blue*
7		What does invisible mean?	*You can't see it*
8		What is the Sun made of?	*Burning gas*
9		What cylinder is used in pastry making?	*A rolling pin*
10		What is the total of 9, 9 and 9?	*27*

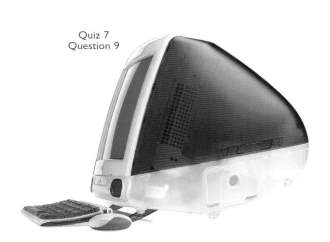

Quiz 7
Question 9

Quiz 7
Question 6

Quiz 9 Level 1

	Questions	Answers
1	What do we measure in litres and millilitres?	*Liquid*
2	What part of your body do you smell with?	*Your nose*
3	What covers more of the Earth: land or sea?	*Sea*
4	Which numbers show on a digital clock at midnight?	*00:00*
5	What is formed when a river flows over a cliff?	*A waterfall*
6	What do we usually call an omnibus?	*A bus*
7	What kind of energy comes into houses through wires?	*Electricity*
8	Which of these shapes would not roll – cylinder, sphere, cuboid?	*A cuboid*
9	What black powder is swept from chimneys?	*Soot*
10	What vehicle rushes emergency patients to hospital?	*An ambulance*

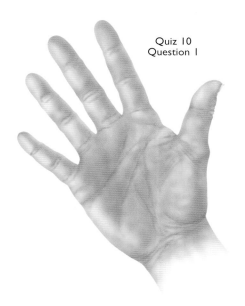

Quiz 10
Question 1

Quiz 10
Question 8

Quiz 10 Level 1

	Questions	Answers
1	What part of your body has a palm?	*Your hand*
2	What food is made from cocoa beans?	*Chocolate*
3	What is the name for a building where things are made?	*A factory*
4	What part of a mountain is the peak?	*The very top*
5	What do you have tested when you go to the optician?	*Your eyes*
6	What should you do before you eat or drink?	*Wash your hands*
7	What are the straight lines light travels in called?	*Rays*
8	Which instrument do we use to measure time?	*A clock*
9	What does water become when it boils?	*Steam*
10	What is the missing number – 2, 4, ?, 8, 10?	*6*

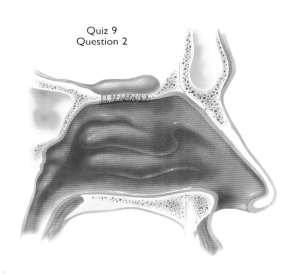

Quiz 9
Question 2

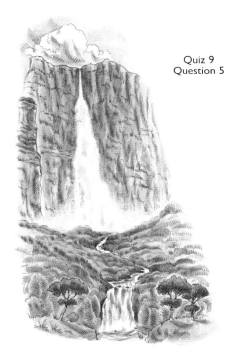

Quiz 9
Question 5

Quiz 11 Level 1

Questions

Answers

		Questions	Answers
1		How is seawater different from fresh water?	*It's salty*
2		In which direction does a compass needle point?	*North*
3		How many hours are there between 10:30 a.m. and 4:30 p.m.?	*Six*
4		What kind of fuel is cut from underground mines?	*Coal*
5		What happens to your face when you blush?	*It turns red*
6		What is raw food?	*Uncooked food*
7		How many lungs do you have?	*Two*
8		Which are the two coldest places on Earth?	*The North and South Pole*
9		What is made when light cannot shine through a solid object?	*A shadow*
10		A right angle is how many degrees?	*90*

Quiz 12
Question 6

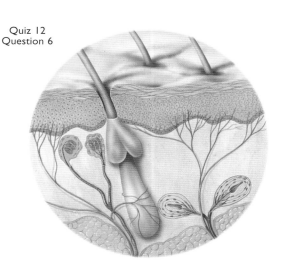

Quiz 12
Question 1

Quiz 12 Level 1

	Questions		Answers
1		Which machine keeps food cool?	*A refrigerator*
2		Which season brings the warmest weather?	*Summer*
3	$\sqrt{x}$	Which will fit together with no spaces in between – circles or squares?	*Squares*
4		How do you produce a sound from a drum?	*By hitting it*
5	$\sqrt{x}$	How many centimetres in half a metre?	*50*
6		What part of your body do you feel with?	*Your skin*
7		What do you find out when you measure how heavy you are?	*Your weight*
8	$\sqrt{x}$	What shape is like a ball?	*A sphere*
9	$\sqrt{x}$	How many days are there in September?	*30*
10		Where would you find your nostrils?	*Your nose*

Quiz 11
Question 4

Quiz 11
Question 2

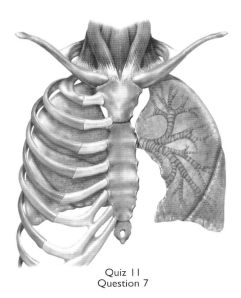

Quiz 11
Question 7

Quiz 13 Level 1

Questions		Answers
1	What is 68 x 10?	*680*
2	Which force pulls everything to the ground?	*Gravity*
3	What is 16 x 5?	*80*
4	What kind of boat can carry cars, trucks and trains across water?	*A ferry*
5	What is the difference between a planet and a star?	*A planet has no heat and light of its own*
6	After the Sun, what is the brightest object in the sky?	*The Moon*
7	What instrument would an astronomer use to look at the stars?	*A telescope*
8	What grows to protect the tips of your fingers and toes?	*Your nails*
9	Do climbing boots have rough or smooth soles?	*Rough*
10	What is ¾ of 100?	*75*

Quiz 14
Question 10

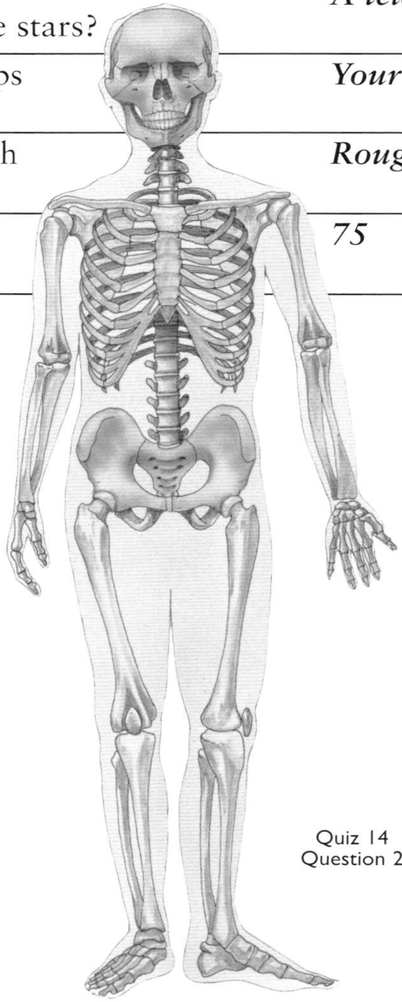

Quiz 14
Question 2

Quiz 14 Level 1

Questions

Answers

		Questions	Answers
1	$\sqrt{x}$	What is ¼ + ¼?	½
2		Your skeleton is made up of 206 what?	*Bones*
3	$\sqrt{x}$	What is the difference between 36 and 60?	*24*
4		What is a Penny Farthing?	*A bicycle*
5		Which hot drink contains caffeine?	*Coffee or tea*
6		What part of your body has a sole?	*Your foot*
7		What material is made from animal skins?	*Leather*
8	$\sqrt{x}$	3D shapes can be measured three ways, how long, how wide and how what?	*High*
9		What shape does a full moon make in the night sky?	*A circle*
10		Is a cello a stringed or a wind instrument?	*Stringed*

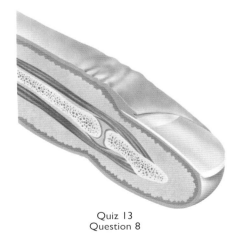

Quiz 13
Question 8

Quiz 13
Question 4

Quiz 15 Level 1

Questions

Answers

		Question	Answer
1		How many grams in half a kilogram?	*500*
2		What is the name of our galaxy?	*The Milky Way*
3		What part of your body does your skull protect?	*Your brain*
4		What is a laboratory?	*A room where scientists work*
5		Which organ pumps blood around your body?	*Your heart*
6		What fills with hot water to heat a room?	*A radiator*
7		What are the roof and walls of a greenhouse usually made of?	*Glass*
8		In 1783, what kind of aircraft carried the first air passengers?	*A balloon*
9		How much of a circle is a semi-circle?	*Half*
10		What is another name for a whirlwind?	*A tornado*

Quiz 16
Question 3

Quiz 16
Question 9

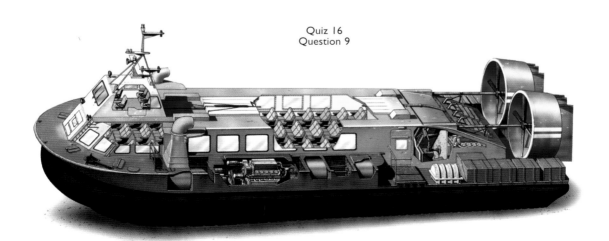

Quiz 16 Level 1

Questions

Answers

		Question	Answer
1	$\sqrt{x}$	In Roman numerals, what is the symbol for zero?	*There is no symbol for zero*
2		Why does an astronaut need to carry oxygen?	*Because there is no air in space*
3		What is the joint that lets you bend your leg?	*Knee*
4		What does an architect design?	*Buildings*
5		What sounds louder, a noise made near or far away?	*A noise made near*
6	$\sqrt{x}$	Which instrument do we use to measure weight?	*Scales*
7		What holds a broken bone in place while it mends?	*A plaster cast*
8		Which of these materials is waterproof: wool, plastic or cotton?	*Plastic*
9		What kind of boat floats along on air?	*A hovercraft*
10	$\sqrt{x}$	What fraction of a cake does each person get if it is divided between 8 people?	*⅛*

Quiz 15
Question 6

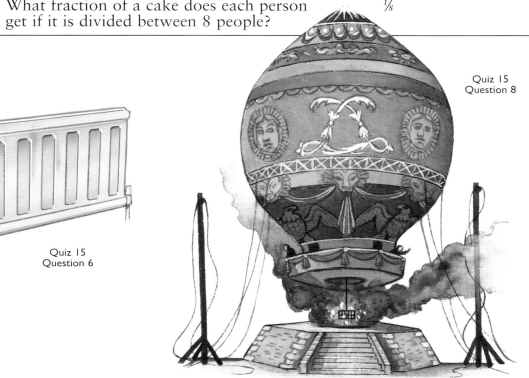

Quiz 15
Question 8

Quiz 17 Level 1

Questions

Answers

#		Question	Answer
1		Which of your five senses do you use to feel a cat's fur?	*Touch*
2		When the Earth shakes violently what is taking place?	*An earthquake*
3		How many tens in 4,260?	*426*
4		What is stronger: a thread of silk or a thread of steel?	*A thread of silk*
5		How many days are there in five weeks?	*35*
6		What is the name for the black and white stripes printed on most of the things we buy?	*The barcode*
7		How many planets are there in the Solar System?	*Eight*
8		What is the joint that lets you bend your arm?	*Elbow*
9		What are bubbles full of?	*Air or gas*
10		What fraction do you need to add to ⅝ to make a whole?	*⅜*

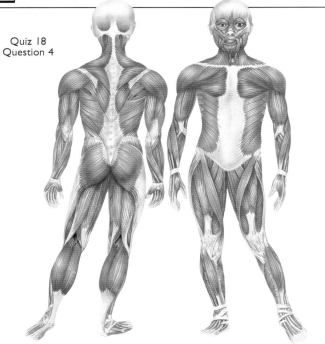

Quiz 18
Question 4

Quiz 18
Question 6

Quiz 18 Level 1

Questions

Answers

		Questions	Answers
1		What supports a building?	*The foundations*
2		What is a shooting star?	*A piece of burning space dust*
3		How many degrees is a whole turn?	*360*
4		What pull your bones and let you move?	*Muscles*
5		Does stainless steel rust?	*No*
6		What is the layer of air around Earth called?	*The atmosphere*
7		If you opened out a cylinder, what shape would it be?	*A rectangle*
8		What are the five senses?	*Sight, hearing, touch, smell and taste*
9		What was Stephenson's *Rocket*?	*A steam train*
10		What does an inventor do?	*Makes something for the first time*

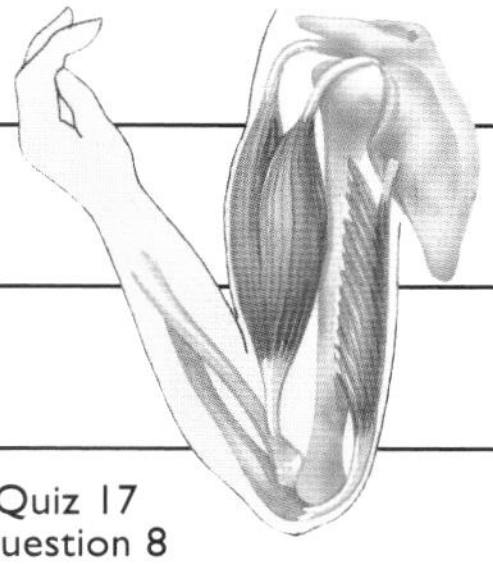

Quiz 17
Question 8

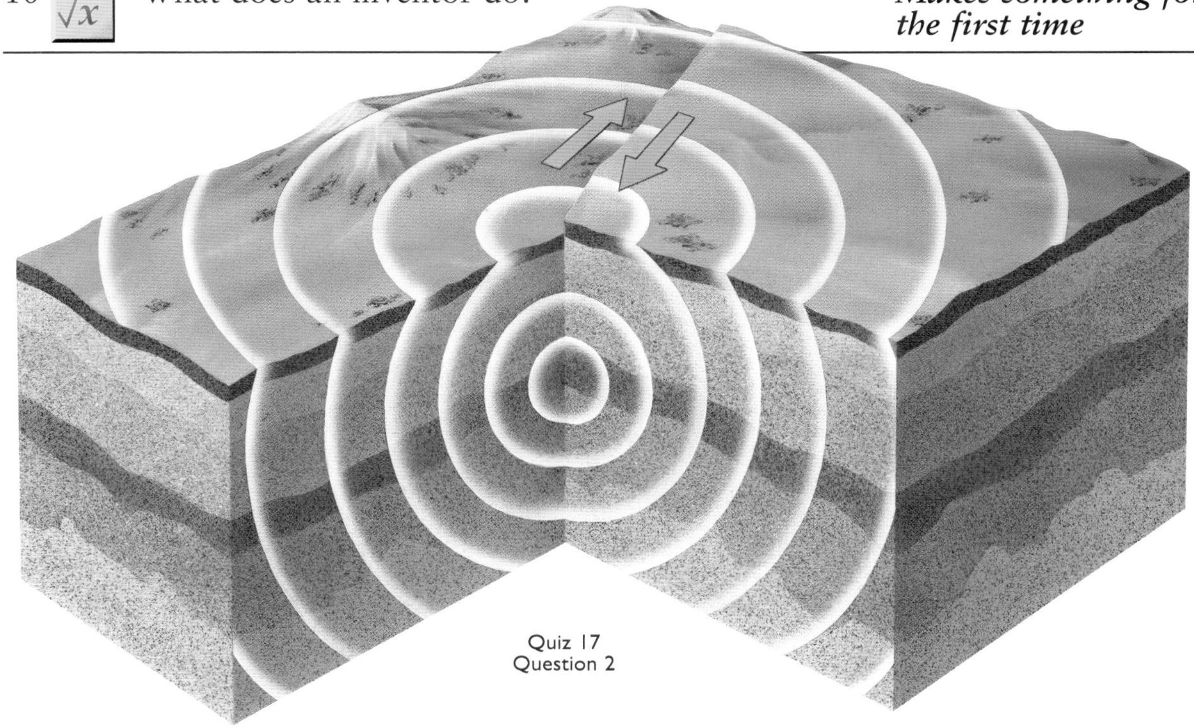

Quiz 17
Question 2

Quiz 19 Level 1

Questions

Answers

		Question	Answer
1		Rubies, diamonds and emeralds are examples of what?	*Precious stones*
2		How many decimetres in a metre?	*10*
3		Which planet is nearest the Sun?	*Mercury*
4		What is the name for the imaginary line around the middle of the Earth?	*The Equator*
5		Where would you find your calf muscle?	*In your leg*
6		Which number divided by six gives six?	*36*
7		What is carried around your body in veins and arteries?	*Blood*
8		What is special about a bicycle called a tandem?	*It carries two riders*
9		Does oil mix with water?	*No*
10		How many metres are there in a kilometre?	*1,000*

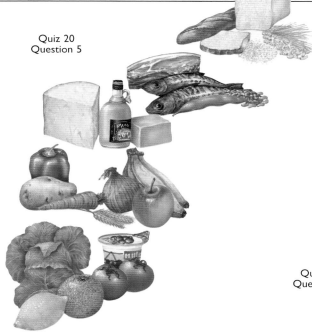

Quiz 20
Question 5

Quiz 20
Question 6

Quiz 20 Level 1

Questions

Answers

		Questions	Answers
1		What has sails that turn round in the wind to work machinery?	*A windmill*
2	$\sqrt{x}$	How many degrees is half a turn?	*180*
3		What is another name for an elevator?	*A lift*
4		A year on Mercury is only 88 days long. True or false?	*True*
5		What gives your body energy?	*Food*
6		Which animals produce silk?	*Silkworms*
7		What do you find out when you take your temperature?	*How hot you are*
8		What does a zoologist study?	*Animals*
9		Which precious stone is green?	*An emerald*
10	$\sqrt{x}$	Does a triangle have any parallel sides?	*No*

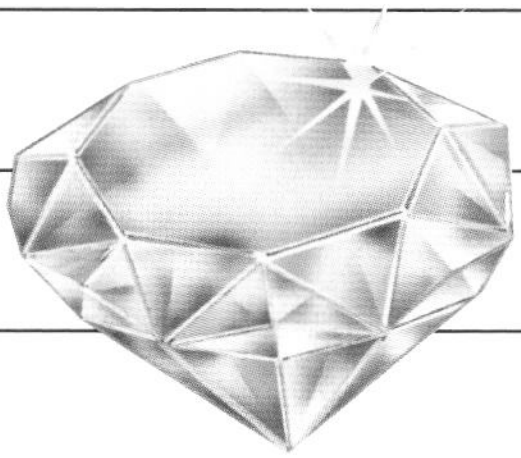

Quiz 19
Question 1

Quiz 19
Question 8

Quiz 21 Level 1

Questions

Answers

		Question	Answer
1		What happens to water at 100°C?	*It boils*
2	$\sqrt{x}$	If today is Wednesday, what is the day after tomorrow?	*Friday*
3		Which is the odd one out – a stethoscope, a thermometer, a magnet, a hammer?	*A magnet is not a doctor's tool*
4		The Sun moves around the Earth. True or false?	*False, Earth moves around the Sun*
5		Which season brings the coldest weather?	*Winter*
6		What takes place in an operating theatre?	*Operations*
7	$\sqrt{x}$	What is the total of 1, 2, 3, 4 and 5?	*15*
8		If something is in motion, what is it doing?	*Moving*
9	$\sqrt{x}$	What is a vertical line?	*A straight line from top to bottom*
10		Which digging machine has a big blade and moves along on crawler tracks?	*A bulldozer*

Quiz 22
Question 7

Quiz 22
Question 9

Quiz 22 Level 1

Questions

			Answers
1	$\sqrt{x}$	How many minutes in a quarter of an hour?	15
2		Where does rubber come from?	*Rubber trees*
3		Where does a subway train travel?	*Underground*
4		What is an avalanche?	*A fall of snow down a mountainside*
5		What is formed when water is surrounded by land?	*A lake*
6		What is a newborn baby's main food?	*Milk*
7		Which will feel hotter after stirring a hot drink – a plastic or metal spoon?	*A metal spoon*
8	$\sqrt{x}$	How much longer is 1 ½ metres than 75 cm?	*75 cm*
9		An object staying on the surface of water is doing what?	*Floating*
10	$\sqrt{x}$	What is the smallest number divisible by both 3 and 4?	*12*

Quiz 21
Question 4

Quiz 21
Question 10

Quiz 23 Level 1

Questions   ## Answers

#		Question	Answer
1	$\sqrt{x}$	What is the total of four 2s and two 4s?	*16*
2		What part of your body has a drum?	*Your ear*
3		What is the name of a little boat that tows a big ship into harbour?	*A tugboat*
4		The fastest trains in the world are powered by steam – true or false?	*False*
5		What would you find in the middle of the Earth?	*Molten rock*
6		What is the largest kind of ship?	*An oil tanker*
7		What fills with air when you breathe in?	*Your lungs*
8		What is the centre of an atom called?	*The nucleus*
9	$\sqrt{x}$	What is the next number in this sequence: 30, 27, 24, 21?	*18*
10		Is cotton a natural or man-made material?	*Natural*

Quiz 24
Question 9

Quiz 24
Question 4

Quiz 24 Level 1

Questions

Answers

		Questions	Answers
1		Iron, steel and copper are examples of what?	*Metal*
2		Who of these does not work in a hospital – paediatrician, nurse, barrister, surgeon?	*Barrister*
3		A magnet has an east and west pole, true or false?	*False – it has a north and south pole*
4		What is the name for three babies born at the same time?	*Triplets*
5		What happens to water at 0°C?	*It freezes*
6		What is the name for the strip where an aircraft lands?	*A runway*
7		Which times table are these numbers part of: 14, 28, 49, 56?	*7*
8		What happens to paper and wood when they become very hot?	*They catch fire*
9		How many legs do six spiders have?	*48*
10		What travels faster – light or sound?	*Light*

Quiz 23
Question 3

Quiz 25 Level 1

	Questions		Answers
1	What are Sirius, Betelgeuse and Polaris all examples of?		*Stars*
2	Which of these numbers is not exactly divisible by five: 10, 12, 30, 45?		*12*
3	Thunder and lightning happen at the same time, true or false?		*True*
4	On a compass, which direction is opposite east?		*West*
5	Things become smaller when they are heated, true or false?		*False, they become bigger*
6	What did Louis Braille invent in 1837?	Quiz 26 Question 6	*A raised dot alphabet for blind people*
7	What language can you see but not hear?		*Sign language*
8	Is river water fresh or salty?		*Fresh*
9	What is the part of your leg above the knee called?		*Thigh*
10	Does a geologist study stars, rocks or dinosaurs?		*Rocks*

Quiz 26
Question 2

Quiz 26 Level 1

Questions

Answers

		Question	Answer
1		What shape is the flat base of a cone?	*A circle*
2		What was known as the iron horse when it was first invented?	*A railway engine*
3		Does the Sun rise in the east or west?	*In the east*
4		Does your heart beat faster or slower when you run?	*Faster*
5		What colour do you get if you mix red and yellow?	*Orange*
6		What is a meteorite?	*A rock from space*
7		If you wave your right hand at a mirror, which hand will your reflection wave back?	*Left*
8		What do you have about five million of growing on your body?	*Hairs*
9		Which of these is not a scientist – physicist, taxidermist, biologist, chemist?	*Taxidermist*
10		Which two of these letters have a line of symmetry – A, G, O, F, L?	*A, O*

Quiz 25
Question 6

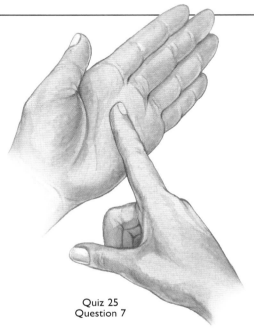

Quiz 25
Question 7

Quiz 27 Level 1

Questions

Answers

		Questions	Answers
1		When animals and clothes are coloured to match surroundings, what is it called?	*Camouflage*
2		What do you see in a planetarium?	*The night sky*
3		Identical twins have the same fingerprints. True or false?	*False*
4		How many sides does a quadrilateral have?	*Four*
5		Where would you find a pupil and an iris?	*In your eye*
6		What colour do you get if you mix yellow and blue?	*Green*
7		If February 2 is a Wednesday, what day will February 6 be?	*Sunday*
8		What kind of work does a machine called an excavator do?	*Digging*
9		How many zeroes are there in twenty thousand?	*Four*
10		What is natural history the study of?	*All living things*

Quiz 28
Question 2

Quiz 28
Question 8

Quiz 28 Level 1

		Questions	Answers
1		How many teeth are there in a full adult set?	32
2		Which planet is well-known for its rings?	Saturn
3		How many faces does a square-based pyramid have altogether?	Five
4		In which season are baby animals usually born?	Spring
5		What part of your body has a lobe?	Your ear
6		What are the seven colours of the rainbow?	R, O, Y, G, B, I, V
7		What is the distance between the centre and the edge of a circle called?	The radius
8		What is the name of a boat that carries cargo along a canal?	A barge
9		How many seconds in 1 ½ minutes?	90
10		What does 'vibrate' mean?	Move fast back and forth

Quiz 27
Question 8

Quiz 29 Level 1

Questions

Answers

		Question	Answer
1		What are the mixture of gases called that come from a car engine?	*Exhaust*
2		What is a monsoon?	*A very heavy rainstorm*
3		Which kind of triangle has three equal sides?	*An equilateral triangle*
4		Your breathe air in through which two parts of your body?	*Your mouth and nose*
5		What colour do you get if you mix red and blue?	*Purple*
6		What are constellations?	*Patterns of stars in the sky*
7		On a 24 hour digital clock, what numbers show at 4 p.m.?	*16:00*
8		At what times of day can the sky become red?	*Sunrise and sunset*
9		What is the total of five 5s and ten 4s?	*65*
10		The artist Leonardo Da Vinci invented a flying machine 500 years ago – true or false?	*True*

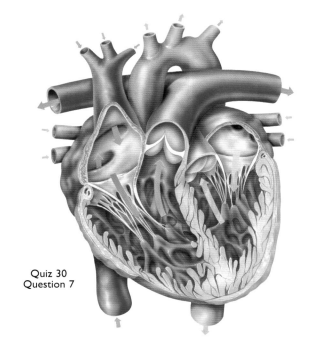

Quiz 30
Question 7

Quiz 30
Question 6

Quiz 30 Level 1

Questions

Answers

		Question	Answer
1	√x	Which kind of clock measures time by the Sun?	*A sundial*
2		What is another name for perspiration?	*Sweat*
3		What is the name for pieces of ice falling from clouds?	*Hail*
4	√x	Which numbers show on a digital clock at a quarter to 11?	*10:45*
5		What is the band of stars we call the Milky Way?	*The edge of our galaxy*
6		Which invention was first called a phonograph?	*A gramophone*
7		What part of your body works like a pump?	*Your heart*
8		Which word describes how loud a sound is?	*Volume*
9	√x	How many degrees is an eighth of a circle?	*45*
10		What do you do to food to fry it?	*Cook it in hot oil*

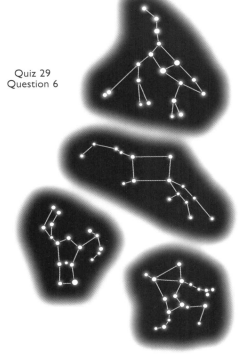

Quiz 29
Question 6

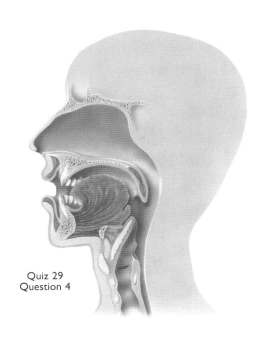

Quiz 29
Question 4

Quiz 31 Level 1

Questions | ## Answers

		Question	Answer
1		How many right angles does a right-angle triangle have?	*One*
2		Which machine is said to work like an electronic brain?	*A computer*
3		Which is the largest planet in the Solar System?	*Jupiter*
4		What is the perimeter of a square with six centimetre sides?	*24 cm*
5		Where in your body is the cerebellum?	*The brain*
6		What silver metal is inside a thermometer?	*Mercury*
7		What is the chemical symbol for lead?	*Pb*
8		Which modelling material is made from newspaper, flour and water?	*Papier mâché*
9		How many minutes long is a TV programme starting at 6:15 and ending at 6:45?	*30*
10		What part of the earth does a scuba diver explore?	*Under the water*

Quiz 32
Question 10

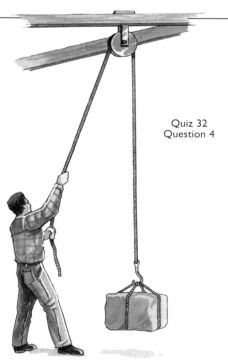

Quiz 32
Question 4

Quiz 32 Level 1

Questions	Answers
1 When a dentist extracts a tooth, what does she do?	She pulls it out
2 What is the name of a giant wave caused by an earthquake?	A tsunami
3 What is ³⁄₁₀ as a decimal?	0.3
4 What is the name for a machine made of ropes and wheels used to lift heavy loads?	A pulley
5 What shape is the moon a few days after a new moon?	A crescent
6 What does your body need eight hours of every day?	Sleep
7 Do you get goose pimples when you are hot or cold?	Cold
8 What is charcoal?	Partly burnt wood
9 What is the name for any flat shape with three or more straight sides?	A polygon
10 What makes a car tyre grip the road?	The tread

Quiz 31
Question 3

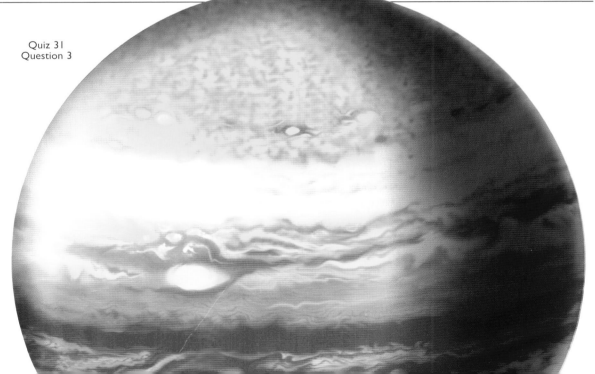

Quiz 33 Level 1

Questions

Answers

		Questions	Answers
1		Is plastic a natural or man-made material?	*Man-made*
2		People never stop growing taller. True or false?	*False*
3		In which season do leaves fall from trees?	*Autumn*
4	$\sqrt{x}$	Which of these numbers can be divided by 5 and 3: 9, 20, 27, 30?	*30*
5		What is a hospital room with several beds called?	*A ward*
6		Which planet was classified as a dwarf planet in 2006?	*Pluto*
7		What does transparent mean?	*See-through*
8	$\sqrt{x}$	Shapes can be 2D or 3D. What does 'D' stand for?	*Dimensions*
9		What is the name for a rod that is used for moving something heavy?	*A lever*
10	$\sqrt{x}$	How much lighter in grams is ½ kilogram than ¾ kilogram?	*250 g*

Quiz 34
Question 6

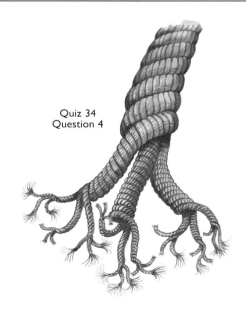

Quiz 34
Question 4

Quiz 34 Level 1

	Questions	Answers
1	Natural wool is waterproof – true or false?	*True*
2	Is the North Pole on land or frozen water?	*Frozen water*
3	What appears on your skin when you get a hard knock?	*A bruise*
4	Long fibres twisted together make a strong what?	*Rope*
5	How many legs does a football team have?	*22*
6	When something spins, how does it move?	*Around and around*
7	What do radios and televisions have for picking up signals?	*An aerial (or antenna)*
8	What is the remainder when 48 is divided by 7?	*Six*
9	What part of the body would a dermatologist treat?	*Skin*
10	Where is rain formed?	*In clouds*

Quiz 33
Question 9

Quiz 33
Question 6

Quiz 35 Level 1

Questions

Answers

		Question	Answer
1		Which does not have a tail: a kite, a boat or an aeroplane?	*A boat*
2		What instrument is used for drawing circles?	*A compass*
3		Does a meteorologist study meteorites, the ocean or the weather?	*The weather*
4		Which gas does fire need to burn?	*Oxygen*
5		How many seconds are there in three minutes?	*180*
6		What is used to stop machine parts rubbing together?	*Oil*
7		What part of your body wrinkles when you frown?	*Your forehead*
8		Earth travels through space at 107,200 kilometres per hour. True or false?	*True*
9		If you had hay fever, what would you be allergic to?	*Pollen*
10		Which angle is greater, a 45° angle or a 90° angle?	*A 90° angle*

Quiz 36
Question 3

Quiz 36
Question 1

Quiz 36 Level 1

Questions   Answers

1. What has hands, a face and wheels? — *A clock*

2. What did Clarence Birdseye develop in 1924? — *Frozen food*

3. What is the name of a giant block of ice floating in the sea? — *An iceberg*

4. Why is blinking good for your eyes? — *It keeps them clean*

   Quiz 35 Question 2

5. What are the two passages in your nose called? — *Nostrils*

6. Do all metals melt when they are hot? — *Yes*

7. When something ignites, what happens to it? — *It catches fire*

8. What is the name for walls of rock that go down to the sea? — *Cliffs*

9. How many centimetres are there in 1 ½ metres? — *150*

10. What is the total of three 3s and seven 4s? — *37*

Quiz 35 Question 9

Quiz 35 Question 4

Quiz 37 Level 1

Questions

Answers

1	What do vaccinations protect you from?	*Infectious diseases*
2	Does electricity flow through metal or rubber?	*Metal*
3	What makes a jack-in-the-box jump out of its box?	*A spring*
4	Put these numbers in order starting with the smallest – 532, 629, 423.	*423, 532, 629*
5	Are the letters on a computer keyboard lower case or upper case?	*Upper case*
6	What do we call the imaginary points at either end of the Earth?	*North and South Poles*
7	Which end of binoculars do you look through to make things look further away?	*The wide end*
8	On which continent would you find zebras and elephants?	*Africa*
9	What is 0.25 as a fraction?	*¼*
10	Is sound a form of energy?	*Yes*

Quiz 38
Question 1

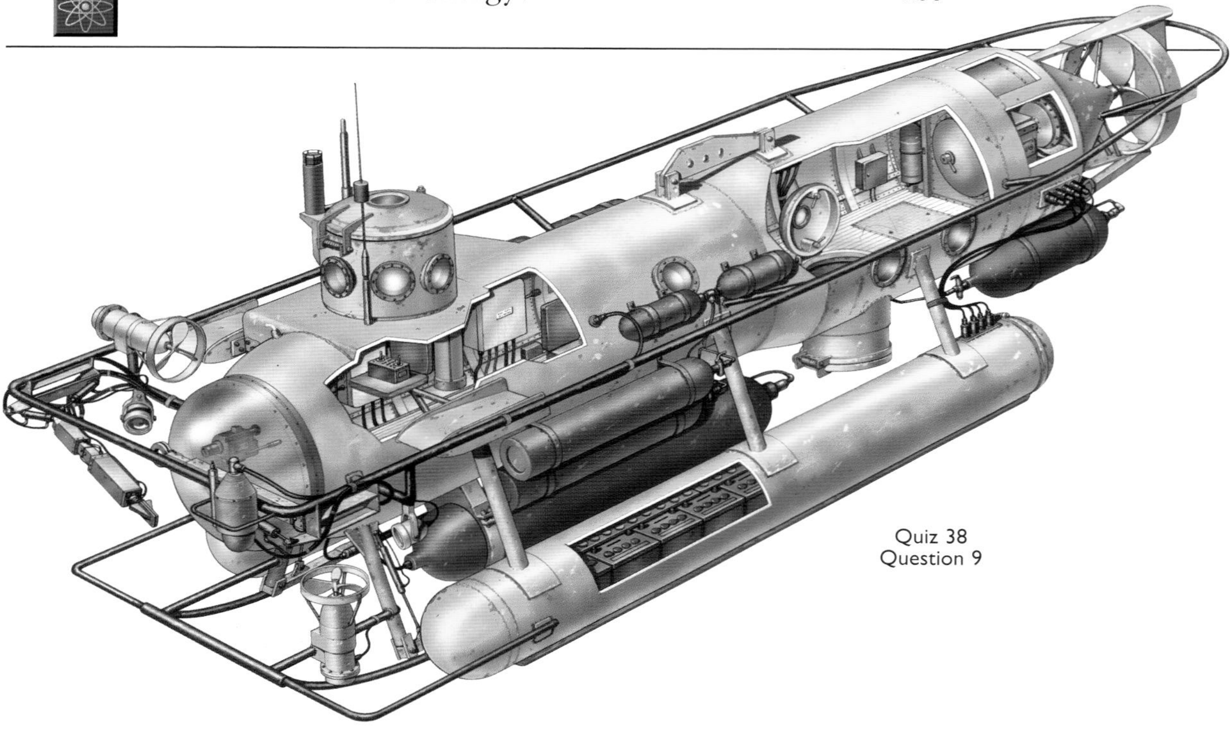

Quiz 38
Question 9

Quiz 38 Level 1

Questions

Answers

		Questions	Answers
1		What is the curved glass in spectacles called?	*A lens*
2		What black powder did the Chinese invent to make fireworks?	*Gunpowder*
3		What is 50% of 80?	*40*
4		How would you describe a material that stretches when it is pulled?	*Elastic*
5		Which number is not exactly divisible by 7: 7, 17, 21, 14, 28?	*17*
6		What would you lose if you had laryngitis?	*Your voice*
7		What in space is an enormous collection of stars?	*A galaxy*
8		What colour is crimson?	*Deep red*
9		Is a bathyscaphe used to explore underground, under the sea or outer space?	*Under the sea*
10		What is the remainder when 26 is divided by 3?	*Two*

Quiz 37
Question 7

Quiz 37
Question 3

Quiz 39 Level 2

Questions

Answers

		Questions	Answers
1		Would you be lighter or heavier on the Moon?	*Lighter*
2		What is the odd one out – rake, hoe, hammer or trowel?	*Hammer*
3		What part of your body would be infected if you had pneumonia?	*Your lungs*
4		What did the first men on the Moon leave behind?	*The American flag*
5		Which metal is used in electric wires – copper or iron?	*Copper*
6		What is the missing number – 18 x ? = 180	*10*
7		Which aircraft with wings has no engine?	*A glider*
8		Which is bigger – an electron or an atom?	*An atom*
9		What is the shortest route from one point to another?	*A straight line*
10		What do you feel when you touch your pulse?	*Your heartbeat*
11		Which 2D shape has five sides?	*A pentagon*
12		What does a biologist study?	*Plants and animals*
13		At the seaside, what are sometimes called white horses?	*White frothy tips of waves*
14		What is the perimeter of a shape?	*Its outside edge*
15		Which precious stone is the hardest material in the world?	*A diamond*

Quiz 40
Question 7

Quiz 40
Question 9

Quiz 40 Level 2

	Questions	Answers
1	Which numbers between 0 and 13 are impossible to get with a throw of two dice?	*1 and 13*
2	What part of your body would conjunctivitus turn red?	*Your eyes*
3	Which number *Apollo* took the first men to the Moon?	*11*
4	What are detergents used to remove?	*Dirt and grease*
5	Which planet is named after the Roman god of war?	*Mars*
6	On a telephone, which number is marked with a raised dot?	*5*
7	Does a palaeontologist study plants, fossils or planets?	*Fossils*
8	How many years are there in a century?	*100*
9	What has a viewfinder, a lens and a shutter?	*A camera*
10	When shapes tessellate, what do they do?	*They fit together*
11	Which natural liquid is used to make nylon?	*Oil*
12	Which part of your body has buds?	*Your tongue*
13	What is used to attach a door to its frame but lets it open and close?	*A hinge*
14	What direction is the opposite to clockwise?	*Anticlockwise*
15	What colour is aquamarine?	*Blue-green*

Quiz 39
Question 7

Quiz 39
Question 11

Quiz 41 Level 2

Questions

Answers

		Questions	Answers
1		Who works with a drill, a mirror and a bright lamp?	*A dentist*
2		What is the missing number: 70 ÷ ? = 10?	*7*
3		Who was the first man on the Moon?	*Neil Armstrong*
4		Which vitamin is found in oranges and lemons?	*C*
5		What are antiseptics used to destroy?	*Germs*
6		What colour is indigo?	*Violet blue*
7		What is the odd one out – duster, broom, spade, mop?	*Spade – the others are for cleaning*
8		What shape is a pie chart?	*Circular*
9		What is an escalator?	*A moving staircase*
10		Which giant creatures lived in the Jurassic period?	*Dinosaurs*
11		Which planet is named after the Roman goddess of love?	*Venus*
12		What is your body mostly made up of?	*Water*
13		At what time of day is your shadow shortest?	*Midday*
14		Which shaped base do the Egyptian pyramids have?	*A square*
15		How many centimetres in are there in 1.8 m?	*180*

Quiz 42
Question 2

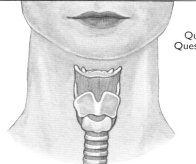

Quiz 42
Question 13

Quiz 42
Question 9

Quiz 42 Level 2

Questions

Answers

		Questions	Answers
1		Which does not travel in waves – light, smells or sound?	*Smells*
2		Which tool is used to grip and pull small objects?	*Pliers*
3		Does carbon dioxide or carbon monoxide make the fizz in fizzy drinks?	*Carbon dioxide*
4		What is the smallest number of cubes needed to build a cube?	*8*
5		On a computer keyboard, which keys change lower case letters to capital letters?	*The shift key and the caps lock key*
6		Do things float more easily in fresh or salty water?	*Salty water*
7		What is the missing sign: 3 ? 9 = 27	*x*
8		What diet does a carnivore have?	*It eats meat*
9		Where does an astronomer work?	*An observatory*
10		What happens at a launch pad?	*Rockets take off into space*
11		During a solar eclipse, what cannot be seen?	*The Sun*
12		Where is the line of symmetry on your body?	*Down the middle from top to bottom*
13		What is another name for your larynx?	*Voice box*
14		How many days altogether in August and September?	*61*
15		If you take medicine orally, how do you take it?	*By mouth*

Quiz 41 Question 11

Quiz 41 Question 8

Quiz 41 Question 10

Quiz 43 Level 2

Questions

Answers

		Questions	Answers
1		What does the word 'dental' refer to?	*Teeth*
2	$\sqrt{x}$	Which curved shape might you find on some shells?	*A spiral*
3		Who works with a stethoscope, a thermometer and an otoscope?	*A doctor*
4		Which of these foods tastes bitter – orange juice, coffee, dark chocolate or milk?	*Coffee, dark chocolate*
5		What does the word 'pitch' describe about a sound?	*How high or low it is*
6		Which flying machine has rotor blades instead of wings?	*A helicopter*
7	$\sqrt{x}$	How many years in a millennium?	*1,000*
8		What is a catamaran – a truck, a sailing boat or a kind of bridge?	*A sailing boat*
9		Which of these materials is not absorbent – towelling, cotton wool, cellophane or tissue?	*Cellophane*
10	$\sqrt{x}$	What is the missing sign: 45 ? 9 = 5	*÷*
11		Which is harder, an emerald or a diamond?	*A diamond*
12		What does the word 'lunar' mean?	*Of the Moon*
13		Which is the odd one out – a torch, a light bulb, a mirror or the Sun?	*A mirror, as it does not give out light*
14		What does rotation mean?	*Turning around like a wheel*
15	$\sqrt{x}$	What is another name for your spine?	*Backbone*

Quiz 44
Question 8

Quiz 44
Question 6

Quiz 44
Question 2

Quiz 44 Level 2

Questions

Answers

#	Question	Answer
1	Which of these materials is not a kind of plastic – acrylic, polythene, concrete, polystyrene?	*Concrete*
2	What is the tallest machine at work on a building site?	*A tower crane*
3	Is a shape with two halves exactly the same symmetrical or asymmetrical?	*Symmetrical*
4	Does your oesophagus lead to your stomach or to your lungs?	*Stomach*
5	What does 'QWERTY' refer to?	*A computer's keyboard layout*
6	Which vegetable can bring tears to your eyes?	*An onion*
7	What is like a big dirty snowball in space?	*A comet*
8	What instrument do scientists use to look at micro-organisms?	*A microscope*
9	Which former planet was discovered in 1930?	*Pluto*
10	What is the perimeter of a regular hexagon with each side measuring 6 cm? Quiz 43 Question 15	*36 cm*
11	What takes a photograph of your bones?	*An X-ray machine*
12	How many pairs of ribs do you have?	*12*
13	The seven colours of the spectrum combine to make what colour light?	*White light*
14	Which part of a circle is the circumference?	*The outside edge*
15	If something accelerates, what is it doing?	*Getting faster*

Quiz 43
Question 6

Quiz 43
Question 12

Quiz 45 Level 2

Questions

Answers

1	What do opposite sides of a die always add up to?	*7*
2	Which of these foods taste sour – vinegar, grapes, lemon, bread?	*Lemon, vinegar*
3	What does the word 'mobile' mean in a 'mobile phone'?	*You can carry it around*
4	Which kind of wheels swivel in all directions?	*Castors*
5	What is heavier – a pound or a kilogram?	*A kilogram*
6	When plants or animals become extinct, what happens to them?	*They die out completely*
7	Do your toenails grow about 1 cm, 1 mm or 0.1 mm a day?	*0.1 mm a day*
8	When scientists dissect something, what do they do?	*They cut it open*
9	Which of these words describes burning – combustion or combination?	*Combustion*
10	Which number is the base of the decimal system?	*10*
11	Why do astronauts float around inside a spacecraft?	*Because there is no gravity*
12	In what part of your body is saliva made?	*In your mouth*
13	Which travels faster – light or sound?	*Light*
14	Red, yellow and blue are primary colours – what are the three secondary colours?	*Orange, purple and green*
15	What is an abacus?	*A counting frame with moveable beads*

Quiz 46
Question 2

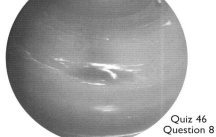

Quiz 46
Question 8

Quiz 46
Question 6

Quiz 46 Level 2

Questions

Answers

		Questions	Answers
1		What did Alexander Graham Bell invent in 1876?	*The telephone*
2		A woolly mammoth was a dinosaur – true or false?	*False, it was a mammal*
3		Which ingredient do all these foods contain – bread, cake, biscuit, pastry?	*Flour*
4		Which sum is the odd one out: 70÷2, 5x7, 25+30, 40–5?	*25+30 does not = 35*
5		Does the Sun rise in Australia before or after it rises in the United States?	*Before*
6		Which boy's name is a machine used to lift cars?	*Jack*
7		Does a computer programmer develop hardware or software?	*Software*
8		Which planet has the same name as the Roman god of the sea?	*Neptune*
9		Where on your body is your skin thickest?	*The soles of your feet*
10		How do you make a sound on a percussion instrument?	*You bang or rattle it*
11		How many seconds in five minutes?	*300*
12		Does shivering warm you up or cool you down?	*Warm you up*
13		Which two numbers come next: 24, 30, 36, 42, ?, ?	*48, 54*
14		Which natural material does a potter work with?	*Clay*
15		What colour is mahogany?	*Dark brown*

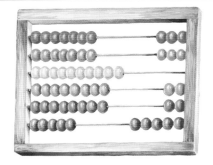

Quiz 45
Question 15

Quiz 45
Question 1

Quiz 47 Level 2

Questions

Answers

		Question		Answer
1		What is a glacier?		*A river of ice and snow*
2		Which is the odd one out – lungs, heart, ribs or brain?		*Ribs, they are not an organ*
3		Which fastener has interlocking teeth?		*A zip*
4		What vibrates on a violin to make a sound?		*Strings*
5		How many minutes between 10 past 5 and twenty to 6?		*30*
6		Who uses a protractor, a compass and a calculator?		*A mathematician*
7		If you owned a PC, what would you have?		*A personal computer*
8		What information does a speedometer give you?		*The speed you are travelling at*
9		What do we call the place where the land meets the sea?		*The coast*
10		What is half of one quarter?		*⅛*
11		A, B, O and AB are types of what?		*Blood*
12		In what part of an aircraft does a pilot sit?		*The cockpit*
13		How many kidneys do you have?		*Two*
14		What are tall metal towers that hold electric cables in the air called?		*Pylons*
15		Will the sum of three even numbers be odd or even?		*Even*

Quiz 48
Question 7

Quiz 48
Question 2

Quiz 48
Question 3

Quiz 48 Level 2

	Questions	Answers
1	What happens to a solid at melting point?	*It turns into a liquid*
2	Which heavy weight stops a ship from drifting away?	*An anchor*
3	What vibrates on a drum to make a sound?	*The skin*
4	How many seconds are there in a minute and a quarter?	*75*
5	Which farm vehicle is used to pull a plough?	*A tractor*
6	Which is the only planet named after a female figure?	*Venus*
7	An oboe, a clarinet and a trumpet are examples of what?	*Wind instruments*
8	What are sick or wounded people carried on in an emergency?	*A stretcher*
9	What does 'recycling' mean?	*Using something again*
10	What is the hole in your eye that lets in light called?	*Pupil*
11	When something expands, what happens to it?	*It becomes bigger*
12	Which metric unit would you use to measure the distance between London and Glasgow?	*Kilometres*
13	What is the word 'lab' short for?	*Laboratory*
14	Does the greenhouse effect make Earth warmer or colder?	*Warmer*
15	Which gas does your body need in order to survive?	*Oxygen*

Quiz 47
Question 1

Quiz 47
Question 4

Quiz 49 Level 2

	Questions	Answers
1	What did alchemists try to turn ordinary metals into?	*Gold*
2	What is ¼ of 28?	*7*
3	If something contracts, does it get bigger or smaller?	*Smaller*
4	Which household machine has a rotating drum, a motor and a water outlet?	*A washing machine*
5	What vibrates inside a flute to make a sound?	*Air*
6	Which is the odd one out – cement, sand, putty or glue?	*Sand does not stick things together*
7	What is 9.35 + 1.45?	*10.8*
8	How many seconds in ¼ of a minute?	*15*
9	What kind of vehicle is used for the radar warning system AWACS?	*Aeroplane*
10	There is no sound in space. True or false?	*True*
11	What is wind?	*Moving air*
12	Which bones protect your lungs?	*Your ribs*
13	What do we call someone who is fully grown?	*An adult*
14	What kind of energy is solar energy?	*Energy from the Sun*
15	What kind of pollution falls from the clouds?	*Acid rain*

Quiz 50
Question 9

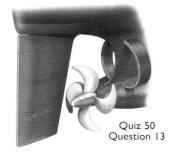

Quiz 50
Question 13

Quiz 50
Question 10

Quiz 50 Level 2

Questions

Answers

		Questions	Answers
1		How many hundreds are there in two thousand five hundred?	25
2		What kind of science is about building machines?	*Technology*
3		Which is bigger, a river or a stream?	*A river*
4		What is more, ¼ or ⅛?	*¼*
5		Does a light bulb give out heat as well as light?	*Yes*
6		The temperature is –4°C. How many degrees must it rise to reach 6°C?	*10°*
7		Why is stainless steel good for making cutlery?	*It doesn't rust*
8		Is your stomach above or below your intestines?	*Above*
9		Which instrument is used to measure angles?	*Protractor*
10		What, in terms of computers, is the monitor?	*The computer's screen*
11		Which is longer, your small or large intestine?	*Small*
12		How long does it take for the Earth to spin around once?	*24 hours*
13		Propellers drive ships and boats through water. True or false?	*True*
14		What is the perimeter of a 6 x 6 cm square?	*24 cm*
15		What part of a car slows it down and stops it?	*The brakes*

Quiz 49
Question 4

Quiz 49
Question 9

Quiz 51 Level 2

Questions

Answers

		Questions	Answers
1		How many days are there in a leap year?	*366*
2		Planets go around the Sun in different directions. True or false?	*False*
3		What do you hear and see in a thunderstorm?	*Thunder and lightning*
4		How many months does a baby take to grow in its mother's womb?	*9*
5		Cold air rises. True or false?	*False, hot air rises*
6		When you are running, do you breathe faster or slower than normal?	*Faster*
7		Will circles tessellate?	*No*
8		How do you make a sound on a percussion instrument?	*You bang or rattle it*
9		What is equal in a regular polygon?	*The sides and angles*
10		What was the first kind of wheel?	*A potter's wheel*
11		Tissue, newsprint and cardboard are examples of what?	*Paper*
12		What kind of oven cooks food with invisible waves?	*A microwave oven*
13		A GP is a kind of doctor – what does it stand for?	*General Practitioner*
14		If you mixed paint of every colour, what colour would you get?	*Brown*
15		Which garden machine has rotating blades and a roller?	*A lawn mower*

Quiz 52
Question 12

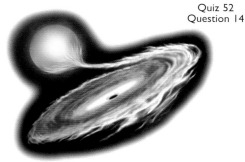

Quiz 52
Question 14

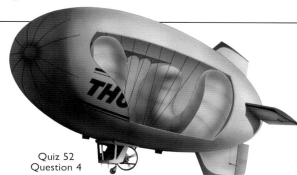

Quiz 52
Question 4

Quiz 52 Level 2

Questions   ## Answers

#	Question	Answer
1	What won't an extinct volcano ever do?	*Erupt*
2	What must you do to a solid to turn it into a liquid?	*Heat it*
3	Which is the longest bone in your body?	*Thighbone*
4	What is a long rod that connects two wheels on a car called?	*An axle*
5	Which part of your body helps you to keep your balance?	*Your ears*
6	What is an example of natural electricity?	*Lightning*
7	In a circle, which line is twice the length of the radius?	*The diameter*
8	How many edges does a square-based pyramid have?	*Eight*
9	Where is the eye of a storm?	*In the centre*
10	How many sides does a nonagon have?	*Nine*
11	What is 'ro-ro' short for when used to describe a ferry?	*Roll-on, roll-off*
12	Which 2D shape has 6 sides?	*A hexagon*
13	Which planet has a moon called Europa?	*Jupiter*
14	In space, what sucks everything into itself, even light?	*A black hole*
15	What is Bill Gates famous for creating?	*Computer software*

Quiz 51
Question 8

Quiz 51
Question 15

Quiz 51
Question 12

Quiz 53 Level 2

Questions

Answers

		Questions	Answers
1		Is it colder at the North or South Pole?	*The South Pole*
2		James Hargreaves invented the 'Spinning Jenny'. What job did it do?	*It spun cotton into thread*
3		What does a compass needle always point towards?	*The north*
4		What are the four seasons? Spring, summer...	*Autumn and winter*
5		The brain is part of the central nervous system – true or false?	*True*
6		What is added to bread dough to make it rise?	*Yeast*
7		Which spacecraft can go into space and come back to Earth again and again?	*Space shuttle*
8		Which force holds us onto the Earth's surface?	*Gravity*
9		What are parallel lines?	*Two lines the same distance apart*
10		What is your first set of teeth called?	*Milk teeth*
11		How many kilograms are there in one metric tonne?	*1,000*
12		What is the name of a curved blade that turns over soil?	*A plough*
13		Who made discoveries about gravity by watching an apple fall?	*Isaac Newton*
14		Which piece of kitchen equipment separates larger pieces from smaller ones?	*A sieve or colander*
15		What is 2°C minus 4°C?	*-2°C*

Quiz 54
Question 2

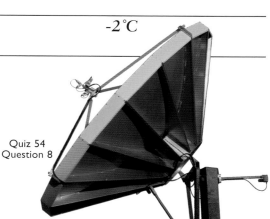

Quiz 54
Question 8

Quiz 54 Level 2

Questions

Answers

		Questions	Answers
1		Which colour is used as a danger warning?	*Red*
2	$\sqrt{x}$	Which shape has its opposite sides equal and parallel?	*A parallelogram*
3		What kind of landscape has very little rain or snow?	*A desert*
4	$\sqrt{x}$	What is added to a year one out of every four years?	*A day*
5		Which is the odd one out – a hole puncher, a paper clip, a stapler, a file? *Quiz 53 Question 6*	*A hole puncher does not hold paper together*
6		What does Ursa Major, the name of a constellation mean?	*Great Bear*
7		Which machine on a building site has a jib, hoist ropes and a hook?	*A crane*
8		What is used to receive signals from a satellite?	*A satellite dish*
9		A supersonic aeroplane flies faster than what?	*Sound*
10	$\sqrt{x}$	How many minutes are there between twenty to 8 and a quarter past 8?	*35*
11		What is the food you eat called?	*Your diet*
12		Which twins look exactly alike – identical or non-identical?	*Identical*
13		What is used to absorb heat from the Sun to make energy?	*Solar panels*
14		What is Earth's natural satellite?	*The Moon*
15		Does a pathologist study disease, navigation or plants?	*Disease*

Quiz 53
Question 7

Quiz 53
Question 3

Quiz 55 Level 2

Questions

Answers

		Question	Answer
1		Is there any kind of life on the Moon?	*No*
2		What is 18 less than 3,004?	*2,986*
3		Which kind of spacecraft orbits the Earth?	*A satellite*
4		What is the hardest substance in the human body?	*Tooth enamel*
5		What does a botanist study?	*Plants*
6		Which flying creatures catch their prey by echo-location?	*Bats*
7		What do we call someone aged between 13 and 19?	*A teenager*
8		Suspension, pontoon and bascule are all kinds of what?	*Bridge*
9		What kind of ships are the biggest in the world?	*Oil tankers*
10		Glass is blown into shape – true or false?	*True*
11		Which is the third planet from the Sun?	*Earth*
12		What is the total of half of 22 and half of 30?	*26*
13		Which insect carries the disease malaria?	*A mosquito*
14		What do the initials 'www' stand for?	*World wide web*
15		What is the odd one out – fresh, frozen, dried or tinned food?	*Fresh food – it has not been preserved*

Quiz 56
Question 9

Quiz 56
Question 13

Quiz 56
Question 5

Quiz 56 Level 2

Questions

Answers

		Question	Answer
1		What do the initials CD stand for?	*Compact disc*
2		How far is 10 times 45 km?	*450 km*
3		Is a laser a fine beam of light or a fine wire?	*A fine beam of light*
4		Is your body is made up of 50%, 70% or 90% water?	*70%*
5		What is the name of the rod a wheel turns round on?	*An axle*
6		Hair and nails are made of dead cells. True or false?	*True*
7		What is a light year?	*The distance light travels in a year*
8		What is the remainder when 240 is divided by 7?	*2*
9		What is a geyser?	*A jet of boiling water from underground*
10		What causes a bruise to turn blue?	*Blood from broken vessels*
11		When desert travellers imagine they see water, what have they seen?	*A mirage*
12		What is bigger – an ocean or a sea?	*An ocean*
13		What is a passenger balloon filled with to make it rise?	*Hot air*
14		What is the place where bones are joined together called?	*A joint*
15		What does a paramedic do?	*Gives out emergency medical care*

Quiz 55
Question 9

Quiz 55
Question 5

Quiz 57 Level 2

Questions

Answers

1. How much is three-quarters of a million? — *750,000*

2. Where are pearls formed? — *In oyster shells*

3. Which imaginary line runs through Greenwich in London? — *The Prime or Greenwich Meridian*

4. How fast is an aircraft travelling at Mach 2? — *Twice the speed of sound*

5. Which of these numbers is not exactly divisible by 9: 27, 45, 21, 90? — *21*

6. Which US president promised to send men to the Moon? — *John F. Kennedy*

7. How many 13s are there is 39? — *3*

Quiz 58 Question 6

8. Which of these materials does not come from an animal – bone, cork, leather, wool? — *Cork*

9. What does a doctor use to listen to your heart and lungs? — *A stethoscope*

10. On what part of your body would you find half moons? — *Your nails*

11. What was a pea souper? — *A thick yellow fog*

12. How long does it take for the Earth to go around the Sun? — *A year*

13. What does the world's most powerful engine drive? — *A rocket*

14. In which two shapes are all four corners right angles? — *Rectangle and square*

15. What word describes a push or a pull? — *A force*

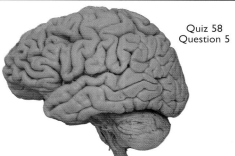

Quiz 58
Question 5

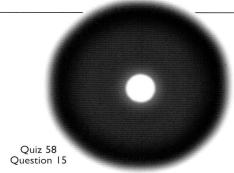

Quiz 58
Question 15

Quiz 58 Level 2

Questions   ## Answers

#	Question	Answer
1	If there is 2 ½ km between your home and school, how far will you travel in a week?	*25 km*
2	In what kind of station is electricity made?	*In a power station*
3	Who studied lightning by flying a kite in a thunderstorm?	*Benjamin Franklin*
4	What is the total of five 8s and three 6s?	*58*
5	What part of your body is sometimes called the control centre?	*The brain*
6	Which transparent material is made from sand?	*Glass*
7	Long ago, which building material was shaped and dried in the sun?	*Bricks*
8	What are biceps, triceps and hamstring examples of?	*Muscles*
9	Which hospital department are patients taken to in an emergency?	*Casualty*
10	What is the biggest kind of storm?	*A hurricane*
11	In Roman numerals, what is 8?	*VIII*
12	Is the Sun higher in the sky at midday in summer or winter?	*Summer*
13	On board an aircraft, what is an autopilot?	*A computer that controls the plane*
14	Which is longer – a mile or a kilometre?	*A mile*
15	Are stars created or destroyed by supernovae?	*Destroyed*

Quiz 57
Question 14

Quiz 57
Question 9

Quiz 59 Level 2

Questions

Answers

		Questions	Answers
1		Which of these two materials will a magnet attract – iron, rubber, gold, nickel?	*Iron and nickel*
2	$\sqrt{x}$	What is ⅓ of 36?	*12*
3		Where are your knuckles?	*On your hand*
4		Which instrument is used to find directions?	*A compass*
5		What does a luminous object give out?	*Light*
6		What oozes from your skin to cool you down?	*Perspiration*
7		What do you call prehistoric plants or animals preserved in rock?	*Fossils*
8		What did John Dunlop invent in 1888?	*The first air-filled tyre*
9		What kind of plants and animals do marine biologists study?	*Sea plants and animals*
10	$\sqrt{x}$	You have 240 ml of milk. How much more do you need to get 370 ml?	*130 ml*
11		What is the name for four babies born at the same time?	*Quadruplets*
12		Which is the second largest planet in the Solar System after Jupiter?	*Saturn*
13		Which tool is used to bore holes?	*A drill*
14		Which stone is used to cut a diamond?	*A diamond*
15	$\sqrt{x}$	Do we use Roman, Arabic or Sumerian numerals today?	*Arabic*

Quiz 60
Question 2

Quiz 60
Question 5

Quiz 60 Level 2

Questions

Answers

		Questions	Answers
1		Which part of the body would a neurosurgeon be likely to operate on?	*The brain*
2		What is the common name for a vent in the Earth that ejects lava?	*Volcano*
3		What are macaroni, tagliatelle and lasagne examples of?	*Pasta*
4		Which part of your body has an arch?	*Your foot*
5		In a submarine, what instrument is used to see above water?	*A periscope*
6		What colour is the semi-precious stone jet?	*Black*
7		What part of a mother does a baby grow in?	*The womb*
8		What is used to make electricity in a hydroelectric power station?	*Water*
9		What grows from your scalp?	*Hair*
10	$\sqrt{x}$	How many 8s are there in 104?	*13*
11		Water on Earth is never lost. True or false?	*True*
12	$\sqrt{x}$	If the perimeter of a square is 32 cm, what is the length of 1 side?	*8 cm*
13		What was the most powerful rocket ever?	**Saturn V**
14		What is used to generate electricity at a tidal power station?	*Rising and falling tides*
15		Saturn's rings are only about 100 m thick – true or false?	*True*

Quiz 59
Question 8

Quiz 59
Question 7

Quiz 59
Question 13

Quiz 61 Level 2

Questions

Answers

		Question	Answer
1		Which code sends messages in long and short beeps or flashes?	*Morse*
2		Who first suggested that humans were related to apes?	*Charles Darwin*
3		Which of these materials cannot be carved – marble, wood, bronze?	*Bronze*
4		What is a quarter of 100?	*25*
5		What gives a bicycle the energy to move?	*A cyclist*
6		Will heated bread melt back into dough?	*No*
7		Where is your Adam's apple?	*In your throat*
8		Which airliner flew faster than the speed of sound?	*Concorde*
9		What are you doing when you exhale?	*Breathing out*
10		Which Ancient Greek scientist discovered how things float while he was in the bath?	*Archimedes*
11		Which side of your brain controls your right hand?	*The left*
12		What do we call the line that is as far as we can see?	*The horizon*
13		What is a comet's tail made up of?	*Gas and dust*
14		Will the year 2012 be a leap year?	*Yes*
15		What is arachnophobia the fear of?	*Spiders*

Quiz 62
Question 4

Quiz 62
Question 2

Quiz 62
Question 12

Quiz 62 Level 2

	Questions		Answers
1		What moves faster than anything else in the universe?	*Light*
2		Which is your index finger?	*Your first finger*
3		How many days are there in 11 weeks?	*77*
4		Which is not a citrus fruit – an apple, an orange or a grapefruit?	*An apple*
5		What do the letters a.m. and p.m. stand for?	*Ante meridiem and post meridiem*
6		Light bends as it passes through water: true or false?	*True*
7		Which is the shortest month of the year?	*February*
8		Where would you find the ozone layer?	*In the Earth's atmosphere*
9		Which scientists study what things are made of and how they react to each other?	*Chemists*
10		What makes the planets shine?	*Reflected sunlight*
11		What is special about a bi-plane?	*It has two sets of wings*
12		Do the thick or thin strings on a guitar play the lower notes?	*Thick*
13		When objects are rubbed together, do they get hotter or cooler?	*Hotter*
14		What is the area of a 12 cm x 12 cm square?	*144 square cm*
15		How is a negative different from a photograph?	*The light and dark areas are reversed*

Quiz 61
Question 8

Quiz 61
Question 10

Quiz 63 Level 2

Questions

Answers

		Questions	Answers
1		What do scientists carry out to test if something is true?	*An experiment*
2		Earth is the only planet with a moon – true or false?	*False*
3		What liquid is made when your mouth waters?	*Saliva*
4		What kind of flying machine was a Spitfire?	*A World War II fighter plane*
5	$\sqrt{x}$	In Roman numerals, what is 1,000?	*M*
6		What is the process called when water goes into the air?	*Evaporation*
7		Who was the first man in space?	*Yuri Gagarin*
8		What kind of vehicle has a conning tower?	*A submarine*
9		What is the word for the Earth's path around the Sun?	*Orbit*
10		Where are the smallest bones in the body?	*The ear*
11		Which part of a light bulb glows?	*The thin wire called a filament*
12	$\sqrt{x}$	How many equal sides does a scalene triangle have?	*None*
13		Which is the human body's heaviest internal organ?	*The liver*
14		What are the cogs on a gear wheel?	*The teeth around the edge*
15	$\sqrt{x}$	How many seconds are there in 3 ½ minutes?	*210*

Quiz 64
Question 8

Quiz 64
Question 4

Quiz 64 Level 2

Questions

Answers

		Questions	Answers
1		What happens to iron if it is left outside?	*It rusts*
2		Is aspirin a painkiller or an antibiotic?	*A painkiller*
3		How do you write a thousandth as a decimal fraction?	*0.001*
4		What happens to light when it shines through a prism?	*It splits into seven colours*
5		If November 3 is a Tuesday, what day was October 29?	*Thursday*
6		If something is buoyant, what can it do?	*Float*
7		What kind of passenger boat has a skirt?	*A hovercraft*
8		Who uses a barometer, a thermometer and an anemometer?	*A meteorologist*
9		What are you doing when you inhale?	*Breathing in*
10		Where would you put a decimal point to make 845 into the smallest number?	*0.845*
11		What is the Beaufort Scale used to measure?	*Wind speed*
12		What is the land between two mountains called?	*A valley*
13		Where are your strongest muscles?	*In your jaw*
14		What kind of spacecraft was *Mir*?	*A space station*
15		What is the name for numbers that can only be divided by themselves and 1?	*Prime numbers*

Quiz 63
Question 7

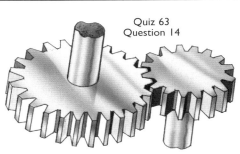

Quiz 63
Question 14

Quiz 65 Level 2

Questions

Answers

		Questions	Answers
1		What is another name for a large hammer?	*A mallet*
2		Which material is made from oil – plastic, glass or rubber?	*Plastic*
3		What is a negative number?	*A number less than 0*
4		What is the name of the machine that weaves thread into cloth?	*A loom*
5		What does the Universe consist of?	*Everything there is*
6		What happens to a boy's voice when it breaks?	*It sounds deeper*
7		What is another word for data?	*Information*
8		When a doctor makes a diagnosis, what is she finding out?	*What is wrong with the patient*
9		Where on your body is your skin the thinnest?	*Eyelids*
10		Which of these shapes is not a polygon – triangle, decagon, tetrahedron or octagon?	*Tetrahedron*
11		What did Edmond Halley have named after him?	*A comet*
12		A bus has 17 seats for 2 and 9 seats for 3, how many passengers can sit down?	*52*
13		What colour does light become when it shines through a green filter?	*Green*
14		Where would you find your canines and incisors?	*In your mouth – they are teeth*
15		Humidity describes how much what is in the air?	*Water*

Quiz 66
Question 5

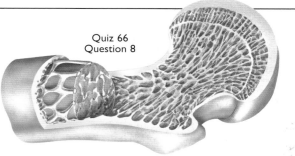

Quiz 66
Question 8

Quiz 66 Level 2

Questions

Answers

		Questions	Answers
1		What was the name of the first artificial satellite?	*Sputnik*
2		What did Charles Macintosh invent in 1823?	*Waterproof material*
3		Does the Moon have weather?	*No*
4		Does it take more muscles to smile or to frown?	*To frown*
5		In which flying machine does the pilot hang below the wings?	*A hang glider*
6		Which times tables are these numbers part of: 200, 50, 40, 110?	*2, 4, 5 and 10 times tables*
7		What foods give you vitamin C?	*Fruit and vegetables*
8		What is the jelly in the middle of your bones called?	*Marrow*
9		Do things look larger or smaller through a concave lens?	*Smaller*
10		In your home, which device breaks an electric circuit?	*A switch*
11		Where would you find a Bunsen burner and a test tube?	*In a laboratory*
12		Which dessert is made from baked whipped egg whites and sugar?	*Meringue*
13		If the perimeter of an equilateral triangle is 21 cm, what is the length of one side?	*7 cm*
14		In Roman numerals, what number does L represent?	*50*
15		What did ancient scientists believe the four elements to be?	*Earth, air, fire and water*

Quiz 65
Question 4

Quiz 65
Question 11

Quiz 67 Level 2

Questions

Answers

		Question	Answer
1		Where would you find the Sea of Tranquility?	*On the Moon*
2	$\sqrt{x}$	What is the total of a quarter of 20 and a quarter of 16?	*9*
3		Is a hologram a 2D or a 3D photograph?	*3D*
4	$\sqrt{x}$	Is a triangle an open or closed shape?	*Closed*
5		In 1962, Telstar sent television pictures from the US to Europe. What was it?	*A satellite*
6		Which machine has one huge, heavy wheel across the front?	*A steamroller*
7	$\sqrt{x}$	How much is half a million?	*500,000*
8		What is special about helicopters and Harrier Jump Jets?	*They take off vertically*
9		What happens to biodegradable material if it is buried?	*It rots away*
10		What is the theory that describes how living things change with time?	*Evolution*
11		What are cirrus, cumulonimbus and stratus all examples of?	*Clouds*
12		What grows from follicles?	*Hair*
13		What are tibia, fibia and cranium examples of?	*Bones*
14		What carries oxygen all around the body?	*Blood*
15		Can light shine through things which are opaque?	*No*

Quiz 68
Question 6

Quiz 68
Question 3

Quiz 68
Question 13

$E=mc^2$

Quiz 68 Level 2

Questions

Answers

		Questions	Answers
1		On a ruler, what is the distance between 35 millimetres and 75 millimetres?	*40 mm*
2		What do long-sighted people see more clearly – things that are near or further away?	*Things that are further away*
3		Which German physicist worked out the theory of relativity?	*Albert Einstein*
4		What is three quarters as a decimal fraction?	*0.75*
5		Does drag slow things down or speed them up?	*Slows them down*
6		Which solid shape has a circular base and a curved surface rising to a point?	*A cone*
7		What carries blood away from the heart?	*Arteries*
8		What is a microchip made of?	*Silicon*
9		Does incoming air pass through your lungs or your windpipe first?	*Windpipe*
10		How do you get energy from coal, oil and gas?	*You burn it*
11		Where would you find black smokers – in a city, on the ocean floor or in a factory?	*On the ocean floor*
12		Which force is produced when two surfaces rub together?	*Friction*
13		What kind of vehicles take part in Formula One Grand Prix races?	*Racing cars*
14		What are intersecting lines?	*Lines that cross each other*
15		What is special about a compass needle?	*It is a magnet*

Quiz 67
Question 5

Quiz 67
Question 8

Quiz 69 Level 2

Questions

Answers

		Questions	Answers
1		Do your back or front teeth grind up your food?	*Back*
2	$\sqrt{x}$	What is 2.3 + 0.7?	*3*
3		What is a vacuum?	*An empty space*
4		What is the name for the study of points, lines, and flat and solid shapes?	*Geometry*
5	$\sqrt{x}$	How many faces does an octahedron have?	*Eight*
6		How did Joseph Lister reduce the number of deaths from surgery?	*He introduced antiseptic*
7		In what industry was William Caxton a pioneer?	*Printing*
8		On a cold day from which part of your body does most heat escape from?	*Your head*
9		Where in the body is the smallest muscle, the stapedius?	*In your ear*
10		What does a geologist study?	*Rocks and how Earth was formed*
11	$\sqrt{x}$	Which of these are square numbers: 9, 25, 14, 21?	*9 and 25*
12		What kind of weather does a tropical rainforest have?	*Hot and wet*
13		What kind of boat has a jib, a mast and a boom?	*A sailing boat*
14		Which force causes the Moon to orbit Earth?	*Gravity*
15	$\sqrt{x}$	How many hundreds are there in a million?	*10,000*

Quiz 70
Question 2

Quiz 70
Question 4

Quiz 70
Question 3

Quiz 70 Level 2

	Questions	Answers
1	How many hours are there in a week?	*168*
2	What do builders use a spirit level for?	*To check if something is level*
3	What kind of boat has wings called foils?	*A hydrofoil*
4	Which husband and wife discovered radium?	*Pierre and Marie Curie*
5	How many degrees colder is -5°C than 1°C?	*6°*
6	What do seismic waves travel through?	*The Earth*
7	What shape is a volcano?	*A cone*
8	What kind of operation is used to give someone a new heart?	*A transplant*
9	What does an angle of 180° look like?	*A straight line*
10	Did Thrust 2 break the land, water or air speed record?	*Land*
11	What happens to sugar and salt when they are mixed in water?	*They dissolve*
12	Air is thinner at the top of a mountain. True or false?	*True*
13	Which two number symbols do binary code use?	*0 and 1*
14	Where in your body would you find a stirrup, hammer and anvil?	*In your ear*
15	Earth is between which two planets?	*Venus and Mars*

Quiz 69
Question 6

Quiz 69
Question 7

Quiz 71 Level 2

Questions | Answers

		Questions	Answers
1		Which scientist wrote *A Brief History of Time*?	*Stephen Hawking*
2		What is 19 in Roman numerals?	*XIX*
3		What can easily happen to inflammable material?	*It can catch fire*
4		What kind of plates is the Earth's surface made from?	*Tectonic plates*
5		What is acoustics the study of?	*Sound*
6		What is the opposite of division?	*Multiplication*
7		Which planet has the most moons?	*Jupiter*
8		How would you arrange these digits to make the smallest number: 5, 1, 8?	*158*
9		Can you hear sounds underwater?	*Yes*
10		What is the study of matter, energy and force called?	*Physics*
11		Which joint lets you move your arm around?	*Your shoulder*
12		Did Alexander Fleming discover aspirin or penicillin?	*Penicillin*
13		What part of the body removes toxins such as alcohol?	*Liver*
14		Which is bigger – a country or a continent?	*A continent*
15		What in centimetres is 75% of 2 metres?	*150 cm*

Quiz 72 Question 4

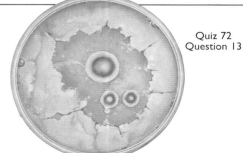

Quiz 72 Question 13

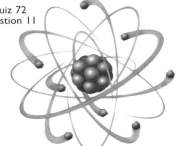

Quiz 72 Question 11

Quiz 72 Level 2

Questions

Answers

		Question	Answer
1		What causes acid rain and smog?	*Pollution*
2		What are aluminium, copper and platinum examples of?	*Metals*
3		What is ⅙ of 30?	*5*
4		What did Thomas Edison invent to light up the dark in 1879?	*The light bulb*
5		Which American brothers made the first successful powered flying machine?	*The Wright brothers*
6		What makes the Moon's craters?	*Meteorites crashing into the Moon*
7		What is the missing number: 70, 63, 56, 42?	*49*
8		Your windpipe connects your mouth with which organs?	*Your lungs*
9		What is the total of three 9s and four 5s?	*47*
10		Which are the last teeth to grow?	*Wisdom teeth*
11		What is everything in the Universe made up of?	*Atoms*
12		What does the word 'science' mean – discovery, knowledge or experiment?	*Knowledge*
13		What was the first antibiotic to be discovered?	*Penicillin*
14		How many degrees each are the angles of an equilateral triangle?	*60°*
15		What is measured in decibels?	*Sound*

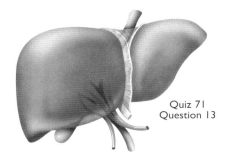

Quiz 71
Question 13

Quiz 71
Question 1

Quiz 73 Level 2

Questions

Answers

#		Question	Answer
1		On a bunsen burner, which is hotter – a blue flame or a yellow flame?	*A blue flame*
2		Which of these foods is not protein – meat, eggs, cabbage, cheese?	*Cabbage*
3		What is 15 less than 4,011?	*3,996*
4		When it is summer in Europe, what season is it in Australia?	*Winter*
5		Do the North poles on two magnets pull together or push apart?	*They push apart*
6		Does an astrologer or an astronomer study the effect of the stars on human lives?	*An astrologer*
7		What are the factors of 22?	*11 and 2*
8		Where on a boat is the outboard engine?	*On the outside of the boat*
9		Do things look larger or smaller through a convex lens?	*Larger*
10		What do anaesthetics stop your body from doing?	*Feeling*
11		What does a food chain always begin with?	*Green plants*
12		What is the name of an angle between 90° and 180°?	*Obtuse*
13		Which road passenger vehicles are powered by overhead cables?	*Trams*
14		What numbers show on a digital clock at a quarter to 9 in the morning?	*08:45*
15		When your bladder is full, what do you want to do?	*Go to the loo*

Quiz 74
Question 14

Quiz 74 Level 2

	Questions	Answers
1	What does the spine protect?	*The spinal cord*
2	Onboard a ship, what is a sextant used for?	*To navigate/ find the way*
3	How many seconds in 10 minutes?	*600*
4	What type of energy is made up of electrons?	*Electricity*
5	What in centimetres is 25% of a metre?	*25 cm*
6	In a car, do you press the brake or the clutch pedal to change gear?	*The clutch pedal*
7	What protects Earth from the heat of the Sun?	*The atmosphere*
8	Is the majority of an iceberg's volume above or below the water's surface?	*Below*
9	Is an alloy a pure or a mixture of metals?	*A mixture*
10	Do you grow more when you are awake or asleep?	*Asleep*
11	If the temperature is 8°C, how many degrees must it drop to reach -2°C?	*10°*
12	What is built in the sea to drill oil from the seabed?	*An oil rig*
13	What is the area of a 12 cm x 12 cm square?	*144 square cm*
14	What kind of vehicle was a Lanchester?	*Car*
15	Is kinetic energy movement or heat energy?	*Movement energy*

Quiz 73
Question 2

Quiz 73
Question 8

Quiz 75 Level 2

Questions

Answers

		Question	Answer
1		What six-sided object does a group of snow crystals form?	*Snowflake*
2		How does a gyroscope move?	*It spins*
3		What are Orion, Cassiopeia and Virgo?	*Constellations*
4		How long does it take for a meal to go through your digestive system – 4 hours, 3 days, 1 week?	*3 days*
5		Steam engines were used to power machines in factories. True or false?	*True*
6		What is special about a Polaroid camera?	*It prints the picture immediately*
7		What is the total of 56, 57, 58 and 59?	*230*
8		Why are there no sounds in space?	*There is no air to carry sounds*
9		How many litres of blood are in an adult's body – 2, 5 or 8?	*Five*
10		How many equal sides does an isosceles triangle have?	*Two*
11		Which metal is a mixture of copper and tin?	*Brass*
12		What is a trawler?	*A fishing boat*
13		What is the study of how plants and animals depend on each other and their surroundings?	*Ecology*
14		What is the name for a solid shape with four or more faces?	*Polyhedron*
15		Which gas do you breathe out – oxygen or carbon dioxide?	*Carbon dioxide*

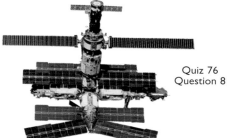

Quiz 76
Question 8

Quiz 76
Question 9

Quiz 76 Level 2

Questions

Answers

		Questions	Answers
1		How many 11s are there in 143?	*13*
2		What did King Camp Gillette invent in 1903 to make shaving safer?	*A safety razor*
3		Where in your body would you find 35 vertebrae?	*In your spine*
4		If there is 2.2 kg in a bag of flour, how much is there in 5 bags of flour?	*11 kg*
5		What device is used to measure the strength of earthquakes?	*A seismograph*
6		Does a conductor let electricity flow, or stop it flowing?	*It lets it flow*
7		Does food pass through the intestines or stomach first?	*Stomach*
8		What, in space, is known as the ISS?	*International Space Station*
9		What kind of arachnid has large pincers and a curved sting on its tail?	*Scorpion*
10		What kind of illness does an oncologist treat?	*Cancer*
11		Does the Moon have an atmosphere?	*No*
12		Onboard a ship, what job does a navigator do?	*Finds the way*
13		Which can flow and has no shape of its own – a liquid or a solid?	*A liquid*
14		What is the area of a 10 cm x 15 cm rectangle?	*150 cm square*
15		In 1895, what kind of show was held in Paris for the first time?	*A film show*

Quiz 75
Question 3

Quiz 75
Question 2

Quiz 77 Level 3

Questions

Answers

		Questions	Answers
1		Which layer of the Earth is directly below the crust?	*The mantle*
2		What part of the human body are digits?	*Fingers and toes*
3		Does a stalactite point up or down in a cave?	*Down*
4		What is half the diameter of a circle called?	*The radius*
5		Who would tell us about isobars and anticyclones?	*A meteorologist*
6		A seesaw is an example of what type of machine?	*A lever*
7		Which is the tallest mountain on Earth?	*Mount Everest*
8		Does salt water freeze at a higher or lower temperature than fresh water?	*Lower*
9		What are the smallest blood vessels called?	*Capillaries*
10		What do we call the long rainy season in India and in some other tropical countries?	*The monsoon*
11		What type of scientist might use a Bunsen burner?	*A chemist*
12		On what type of transport would you find an aileron?	*An aeroplane*
13		How do bats find their way around?	*By echolocation*
14		What is one-half of one-sixth?	*One-twelfth*
15		Where on the body is the cornea?	*The eye*

Quiz 78
Question 14

Quiz 78
Question 2

Quiz 78 Level 3

Questions   ## Answers

1	Cyclones and typhoons are other words for what type of storm?	*Hurricanes*
2	On which part of a shark's body is its dorsal fin?	*Its back*
3	What is the name of the bomb that is launched from a ship to attack a submarine?	*A depth charge*
4	Where is the hard palate?	*The roof of the mouth*
5	You use a pair of what to draw a circle?	*Compasses*
6	What is the name for the explosion that created our Universe?	*The Big Bang*
7	What do Americans call a gearbox?	*A transmission*
8	What happens to an object when it decelerates?	*It slows down*
9	What is a clove hitch?	*A type of knot*
10	Kinetic and potential are types of what?	*Energy*
11	How many half-dozen boxes do you need to collect 40 eggs?	*Seven*
12	What does a palaeontologist study?	*Fossils*
13	What is the pampas of South America?	*Vast grasslands*
14	An astrolabe was an earlier version of which device used in navigation?	*A sextant*
15	Where is your sternum?	*Your chest (the breastbone)*

Quiz 77
Question 12

Quiz 77
Question 13

Quiz 79 Level 3

Questions

Answers

		Questions	Answers
1		What type of power is generated by the force of running water?	*Hydroelectric power*
2		What is a ketch?	*A type of sailing boat*
3		Within which organs are the alveoli?	*The lungs*
4		What is half of a half?	*A quarter*
5		If an engineer works out the elevation of something, what has he or she measured?	*Its height above sea level*
6		What type of machine lifts a car up?	*A jack*
7		What name is given to the curd of milk when it has been squeezed into a solid mass?	*Cheese*
8		What job does a car radiator perform?	*It cools the engine*
9		Which of the following shapes is a quadrilateral – pentagon, triangle, octagon, rectangle?	*Rectangle*
10		What are dark blotches on the Sun called?	*Sunspots*
11		On what type of vehicle would you find a derailleur?	*A bicycle*
12		A tremor is a minor form of what event?	*Earthquake*
13		What is 100 divided by four?	*25*
14		What is the name of the tube that supplies nourishment to a baby in its mother's womb?	*The umbilical cord*
15		The Atacama Desert, the driest place on Earth, is on which continent?	*South America*

Quiz 80
Question 2

Quiz 80
Question 9

Quiz 80 Level 3

Questions

Answers

#	Question	Answer
1	What do Americans call the silencer of a car?	*The muffler*
2	*Archaeopteryx*, which lived at the time of the dinosaurs, was a primitive type of what?	*Bird*
3	What does a botanist study?	*Plants*
4	What name is given to a scientist who studies dinosaurs?	*A palaeontologist*
5	A giraffe has the same number of bones in its neck as a human: true or false?	*True*
6	What do ligaments connect?	*Bones*
7	What is precipitation?	*Rainfall (including frozen types)*
8	What part of a car can come in disc and drum form?	*Brakes*
9	What is the closest living relative to the now-extinct mastodon?	*Elephant*
10	Giant redwood trees are natives of which continent?	*North America*
11	John Logie Baird invented which means of communication?	*Television*
12	What do you do when you square a number?	*You multiply it by itself*
13	How many bits are there in a byte?	*Eight*
14	Which species has the Latin name *Homo Sapiens*?	*Human beings*
15	Can you live without your appendix?	*Yes*

Quiz 79
Question 7

Quiz 79
Question 2

Quiz 81 Level 3

Questions

Answers

		Question	Answer
1		John Glenn became the first American to do what, in 1962?	*Orbit the Earth in a spacecraft*
2		What machine first worked for a living in 1961?	*Robot*
3		What type of animal is a grebe?	*A bird*
4		What is a half plus an eighth?	*Five-eighths*
5		What is the name of the imaginary line around which a ball spins?	*The axis*
6		What sort of region could be described as being arid?	*One that is very dry, such as a desert*
7		The Swedish scientist Anders Celsius invented a method of measuring what?	*Temperature*
8		Which technology began its existence as ARPANET?	*The Internet*
9		Fill in the symbols to complete this sum: 14 ? 6 ? 3 = 17	*+ and -*
10		What kind of vehicle runs on rails on the road?	*A tram*
11		A mile is about 1.6 km. How many kilometres are there in 30 miles?	*About 48*
12		By which informal name is the disease BSE known?	*Mad Cow Disease*
13		Ursa Major, Libra, Casseiopia and Virgo are names for what?	*Constellations*
14		Which organ contains the duodenum, jejunum and ileum?	*The small intestine*
15		What everyday object has a thin coil of wire called a filament?	*A light bulb*

Quiz 82
Question 11

Quiz 82
Question 1

Quiz 82
Question 14

Quiz 82 Level 3

Questions

Answers

		Question	Answer
1		How many legs do all insects have?	Six
2	$\sqrt{x}$	If two angles of a triangle add up to 140 degrees, what must the third angle be?	40 degrees
3		How many teeth are there in a full set of primary ('milk') teeth?	20
4		Which planet has the same name as a type of metal?	Mercury
5		If a material is an adhesive, what does it do?	It sticks things together
6		Why do certain animals have webbed feet?	To allow them to swim faster
7		Which scientist won a Nobel Prize for Chemistry for her work investigating radioactivity?	Marie Curie
8	$\sqrt{x}$	How many eggs are there in six and a half dozen?	78
9		Which type of blood cells carry oxygen?	Red blood cells
10		How much of the Moon is visible during a New Moon?	None (it is all in shadow)
11		What is unusual about the Venus fly-trap and the pitcher plant?	They both trap and eat insects
12	$\sqrt{x}$	Using only the digits 4, 5 and 1, make two even numbers.	154 and 514
13		What were *Skylab* and *Salyut* early examples of?	Space station
14		What is the albumen of an egg?	The white
15		Which muscle is in the back of the leg, below the knee?	The calf

Quiz 81
Question 15

Quiz 81
Question 13

Quiz 81
Question 10

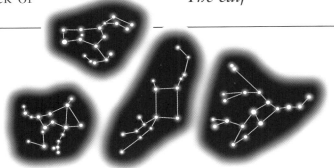

Quiz 83 Level 3

Questions

Answers

1. Astronomers once believed that which planet had canals on its surface? — *Mars*

2. Where would you find a flying jib? — *On a sailing boat (a type of sail)*

3. What does a horticulturist study? — *The way plants can be grown for food*

Quiz 84 Question 12

4. What would a doctor use a sphygmomanometer to measure – height, blood pressure or weight? — *Blood pressure*

5. Two numbers added together make 20, but multiplied together make 91. What are they? — *7 and 13*

6. Which reddish-brown metal is formed into thin wires that conduct electricity? — *Copper*

7. What are Saturn's rings made of? — *Rock fragments*

8. What was the first animal in space? — *A dog called Laika*

9. In 1938, what did German physicists Otto Hahn and Fritz Strassman achieve? — *They split the atom*

10. Which American animal, with a northern and crab-eating variety, has a bushy ringed tail? — *Raccoon*

11. Inches, pounds and miles are all measurements in which system? — *Imperial*

12. What is a gale? — *A very strong wind*

13. What is the name for the body's liquid waste? — *Urine*

14. What is 0.125 as a fraction? — *One-eighth*

15. A toy car travels 30 cm with six wheel turns. How far would it go with four winds? — *20 cm*

Quiz 84
Question 2

Quiz 84
Question 10

Quiz 84 Level 3

Questions

Answers

		Questions	Answers
1		What is 0.75 of 24?	*18*
2		What type of animal is a tarantula?	*Spider*
3		What type of object can be either a red giant, white dwarf or black dwarf?	*A star*
4		Smoking tobacco harms two major organs of the body; one is the lungs, what is the other?	*The heart*
5		How many grams are there in a kilogram?	*1,000*
6		Which grow to be larger – African or Asian elephants?	*African*
7		When you square an odd number, will the result also be an odd number?	*Yes*
8		Which liquid do people put in car radiators to prevent ice from forming in the winter?	*Anti-freeze*
9		What part of the body does arthritis affect?	*The bones*
10		What feature links penguins, rheas, ostriches and kiwis?	*They are all birds that cannot fly*
11		Russia developed the first nuclear weapon – true or false?	*False*
12		Where could you find a stigma, carpels and sepals?	*In a flower*
13		How many weeks are there in five years?	*260*
14		Which planets, apart from Saturn, have rings?	*Jupiter, Uranus and Neptune*
15		Are eggs produced by male or female plants?	*Females*

Quiz 83
Question 7

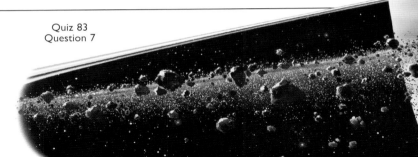

Quiz 83
Question 4

Quiz 85 Level 3

Questions

Answers

		Questions	Answers
1		How many people or things are there in a quintet?	*Five*
2		With what sort of power are the engineers James Watt and Thomas Newcomen associated?	*Steam*
3		Pneumonia affects which part of the body?	*The lungs*
4		Why is an elephant's footprint no deeper than a human's?	*Because its huge foot spreads the weight*
5		Is black ice really black?	*No – it is clear*
6		What sort of scientist would be concerned with isobars, high pressure fronts and occluded fronts?	*Meteorologist*
7		Which is the odd one out: whale, shark, cod, skate?	*Whale (the others are all fish)*
8		What is the total number of spots on a six-sided die?	*21*
9		Which object, used to make things look bigger, can make paper burn?	*A magnifying glass*
10		Which objects in space have tails up to 160 million km long?	*Comets*
11		John Loudon McAdam invented a system for strengthening the surface of what?	*Roads*
12		Iron will only rust if both air and what else are present?	*Water*
13		Who has more bones – a man or a woman?	*They have the same number*
14		Did the United States, China or the USSR send the first satellite into space?	*USSR*
15		Combustion is the scientific word for which process?	*Burning*

Quiz 86
Question 8

Quiz 86
Question 7

Quiz 86
Question 3

Quiz 86 Level 3

Questions

Answers

#	Question	Answer
1	What do these have in common: Appalachians, Dolomites, Urals and Atlas?	*They are all mountain ranges*
2	What is one-fifth of one-fifth?	*One-twenty-fifth*
3	What was *Voyager II*?	*A space probe*
4	What type of person would have to study anatomy and physiology?	*A doctor or surgeon*
5	The human skull is actually made up of 22 separate bones – true or false?	*True*
6	To the nearest 10 million km, how far is the Sun from the Earth?	*150 million km (93 million miles)*
7	What do Americans call a torch?	*A flashlight*
8	How many arms does a starfish have?	*Five*
9	What does the prefix 'iso' mean in the words isosceles and isobar?	*The same*
10	When was the first nuclear weapon tested?	*1945*
11	On which planet is Olympus Mons, the largest volcano in the Solar System?	*Mars*
12	If a doctor gave you an antihistamine, how would you be affected?	*Your nose would become less stuffy*
13	Who invented the first car driven by an internal combustion engine?	*Karl Benz*
14	What is the main ingredient of paper?	*Wood pulp*
15	If you divided a rectangle diagonally, what two shapes would you create?	*Two triangles*

Quiz 85
Question 9

Quiz 85
Question 10

Quiz 87 Level 3

Questions

Answers

		Questions	Answers
1		What word describes the horizontal and vertical lines on a graph?	*Axis*
2		If it is 2 p.m. in London, what time is it in New York?	*9 a.m.*
3		Where in your body are synapses found?	*The brain*
4		What kind of plane was a Lancaster?	*A bomber*
5		If you are looking forward on a ship, which way is starboard?	*To the right*
6		How many millimetres are there in a centimetre?	*Ten*
7		Why do reptiles bask in the sunshine?	*To warm their blood*
8		Alfred Nobel, who founded the Nobel Prizes, invented what in 1866?	*Dynamite*
9		What is a fjord?	*A narrow, steep-sided bay*
10		In which sport would a 'float' be used to indicate a bite?	*Fishing*
11		What word describes a solid shape with circles at each end?	*Cylinder*
12		In which year did Yuri Gagarin make the first manned space flight: 1959, 1961 or 1963?	*1961*
13		What sort of patient would a paediatrician treat?	*A child*
14		What type of animal are vipers, adders and mambos?	*Snakes*
15		What is the normal body temperature of a healthy person?	*37°C (98.6°F)*

Quiz 88
Question 13

Quiz 88
Question 5

Quiz 88 Level 3

Questions

Answers

		Questions	Answers
1		Where would you find the rudder of an aeroplane?	*On the tail fin*
2		What material is used to produce LP records?	*Vinyl*
3		How many hours are there in five days?	*120*
4		On which continent is Angel Falls, the world's highest waterfall?	*South America*
5		What part of a fish aids buoyancy?	*Swim-bladder*
6		What blood problem affects someone with haemophilia?	*The blood does not clot properly*
7		A fuel cell is a type of what? Quiz 87 Question 10	*Battery*
8		What happens when pottery is 'fired'?	*It is baked until it becomes hard*
9		Euclid, the Greek mathematician, is known as the father of what?	*Geometry*
10		How many grams are there in 5 kg?	*5,000*
11		What is smog?	*A mixture of smoke and fog*
12		Which South American animal hangs from trees and seems to spend its whole life sleeping?	*The sloth*
13		What would a serial or parallel cable be used for?	*Connecting devices to a computer*
14		Which type of scientist would study quasars, pulsars and asteroids?	*An astronomer*
15		You would find a cuticle at the base of what parts of the body?	*Fingernails and toenails*

Quiz 87
Question 4

Quiz 89 Level 3

Questions

Answers

		Question	Answer
1		Which fireproof building material can damage the lungs if breathed in?	*Asbestos*
2		A ship's crow's nest is located at the top of what?	*The main mast*
3		What is the more common term for an integer?	*A whole number*
4		How many moons does Uranus have: 7, 27 or 57?	*27*
5		What famous table did the Russian chemist Dmitri Mendeleev produce?	*The periodic table of elements*
6		Where in your body would you find your adenoids?	*At the back of the nose and throat*
7		How many inches are there in 5 feet?	*60*
8		What vehicle was first built in 1936 by Ferdinand Porsche in Germany?	*The Volkswagen Beetle car*
9		Which has more calories per 100 g – butter or milk?	*Butter*
10		What device is used to listen inside the body?	*A stethoscope*
11		What did Tim Berners-Lee invent in 1989?	*The World Wide Web*
12		If it is spring in Canada what season is it in New Zealand?	*Autumn*
13		On which continent would you find orang-utans?	*Asia*
14		What are both the Julian and Gregorian?	*Types of calendar*
15		Which part of the body is affected by eczema?	*The skin*

Quiz 90
Question 10

Quiz 90
Question 7

Quiz 90 Level 3

Questions

Answers

		Questions	Answers
1		How many lines of symmetry does a square have?	*Four*
2		What do you call a rock or mineral from which a metal can be extracted?	*An ore*
3		What is the soft inner part of the bone, where blood cells are made?	*The marrow*
4		If I have 14 sweets and give 3 to one friend and 2 to another, how many sweets do I have left?	*9*
5		If an engineer is measuring the gradient of a hillside, what is he or she finding?	*How steep it is*
6		What type of behaviour is typical of most people suffering from anorexia?	*They only eat tiny amounts of food*
7		What is a boa constrictor?	*A type of snake*
8		What is a gorge?	*A narrow, steep-sided valley*
9		What sort of vehicle would a scientist at Cape Canaveral, Florida, be working on?	*A rocket*
10		What kind of weapons are Berettas?	*Guns*
11		How fast is the Earth orbiting the Sun to the nearest 5,000 km/h?	*107,200 km/h*
12		What insect shares its name with a swimming stroke?	*A butterfly*
13		What does the prefix 'milli' mean in metric measurements?	*One-thousandth*
14		What process causes water droplets to form on a cold window?	*Condensation*
15		The science of the study of the body and its parts is called what?	*Anatomy*

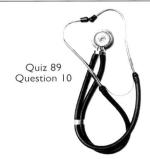

Quiz 89
Question 10

Quiz 89
Question 2

Quiz 91 Level 3

Questions

Answers

		Question	Answer
1		What type of tough string is pulled between the teeth to clean them and to strengthen the gums?	*Dental floss*
2		Which planet is known as the red planet?	*Mars*
3		What does a nutritionist specialize in?	*Food and diet*
4		What is the largest land carnivore in the world?	*Polar bear*
5		Which part of the eye becomes wider or narrower, depending on how bright the light is?	*The pupil*
6		What is acoustics the study of?	*Sound, and how it travels*
7		In Roman numerals, what is CLVI divided by XIII?	*XII*
8		Which kitchen utensil shares its name with a quick, light movement?	*A whisk*
9		What does it mean if an animal is a vertebrate?	*It has a backbone*
10		Which is the body's largest joint?	*The knee*
11		What is the nearest whole number to pi, which is used to measure circles?	*3 (3.14159)*
12		What was the Black Death, which killed millions of people during the Middle Ages?	*Bubonic plague, a deadly disease*
13		Where would you find an estuary?	*At the mouth of a river*
14		In which year did human beings first set foot on the Moon?	*1969*
15		Where would you find a femur bone?	*In your leg*

Quiz 92
Question 4

Quiz 92
Question 1

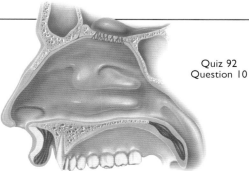

Quiz 92
Question 10

Quiz 92 Level 3

Questions

Answers

#		Question	Answer
1		What is the name for an L-shaped hexagonal rod used to undo a certain type of screw?	*An Allen key*
2		How does eating fibre help the body?	*It helps the body get rid of wastes*
3		What do 25, 16 and 9 have in common?	*They are all square numbers*
4		What shape is a sphere?	*Round, like a ball*
5		What term describes trees that have cones?	*Coniferous*
6		Which animals travel in packs?	*Wolves and wild dogs*
7		What is two-thirds of two-thirds?	*Four-ninths*
8		What part of your body would an optometrist study?	*Your eyes*
9		What is a monocle?	*A lens worn in one eye*
10		What part of the body does nasal refer to?	*The nose*
11		The name of which type of animal means 'terrible lizard' in Greek?	*Dinosaur*
12		What is 75 percent of 444?	*333*
13		Why should people trying to lose weight remove the skin from chicken?	*Because the skin contains the most fat*
14		What is 'flu' short for?	*Influenza*
15		Can bears climb trees?	*Yes*

Quiz 91
Question 8

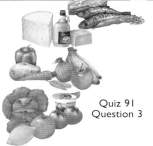

Quiz 91
Question 3

Quiz 93 Level 3

Questions

Answers

		Questions	Answers
1		Rubella is a disease, also called what?	*German measles*
2		How many cards are there in each suit of a deck of playing cards?	*13*
3		In which country did the Industrial Revolution begin in the 1700s?	*Great Britain*
4		On which part of the body is the biceps?	*The upper arm (muscle)*
5		Where do lugworms live?	*In mud by the seashore*
6		Which part of a fraction is the dividend?	*The lower half*
7		True or false: engineers using high-pressure tools can turn copper into gold?	*False*
8		'Rheumatoid' is a type of which bone ailment?	*Arthritis*
9		What is a penny farthing?	*An early type of bicycle*
10		What is made by baking dough?	*Bread*
11		What is at the centre of our Solar System?	*The Sun*
12		When was the first CD sold?	*1982*
13		What type of medical professional removes plaque?	*A dentist or dental hygienist*
14		On which continent would you find coyotes?	*North America*
15		True or false: men have more wisdom teeth than women?	*False, both have four*

Quiz 94
Question 9

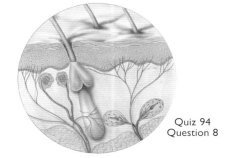

Quiz 94
Question 8

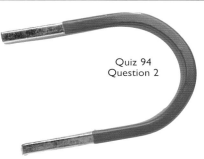

Quiz 94
Question 2

Quiz 94 Level 3

Questions

Answers

		Questions	Answers
1		True or false: scientists have found written messages on the surface of the Moon?	*False*
2		What comes in varieties called bar, horseshoe and electro?	*Magnets*
3		What are stars that orbit the same point or even one another called?	*Binary stars*
4		How many weeks are there in five years?	*260*
5		When water reaches its boiling point, what does it become?	*Steam (water vapour)*
6		Which itchy condition, caused by a fungus, usually affects the area between the toes?	*Athlete's foot*
7		What navigational device uses a magnet suspended or floated in a liquid?	*A magnetic compass*
8		What does a dermatologist study?	*The skin*
9		What name is given to the hairs on a paintbrush?	*Bristles*
10		Where is the spinal cord?	*In your backbone*
11		True or false: special underwater telescopes can provide the clearest images of the Sun?	*False*
12		What is the fastest land animal over a distance of 2 km?	*A thoroughbred horse*
13		What is 20 percent of 20?	*4*
14		True or false: driving a car in reverse saves on petrol?	*False*
15		In which ocean does the Gulf Stream flow?	*The Atlantic*

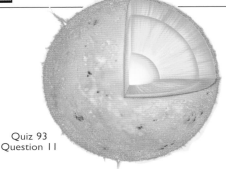

Quiz 93
Question 11

Quiz 93
Question 10

Quiz 95 Level 3

Questions

Answers

		Question	Answer
1		What device for seeing distant objects has a name that means 'for both eyes'?	*Binoculars*
2		What is a dingo?	*A wild dog of Australia*
3		Which fruit's fall to the ground inspired Isaac Newton's theory of gravity?	*An apple*
4		What is a stickleback?	*A type of fish*
5		What is another name for a shooting star?	*A meteor*
6		If a car is travelling at 60 km/h, how far will it go in 15 minutes?	*15 km*
7		What does a barometer measure?	*The pressure of the atmosphere*
8		True or false: biologists have developed redwood trees that can grow in the Sahara?	*False*
9		What is 25% of 16?	*4*
10		What do your olfactory organs allow you to do?	*Detect smells*
11		What type of animals are described as 'equine'?	*Horses and their relatives*
12		What covers more than two-thirds of the world's surface?	*Water*
13		What device for measuring time uses running sand?	*Hour-glass*
14		The core of the Earth is made of nickel and which other element?	*Iron*
15		Is baking powder a type of acid or alkali?	*Alkali (the opposite of acid)*

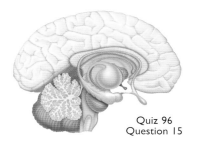

Quiz 96
Question 15

Quiz 96
Question 4

Quiz 96 Level 3

Questions

Answers

		Questions	Answers
1		True or false: the people of Iceland get most of their hot water from hot springs?	*True*
2		In a group of 100 people, how many people are likely to be left-handed?	*Ten*
3		What is 40 percent of 40?	*16*
4		What kind of watch is used to time a race?	*A stopwatch*
5		The grey squirrel is native to which continent?	*North America*
6		Correct to within two minutes, how long does light take to reach us from the Sun?	*Eight minutes*
7		What process causes sounds to be recorded on tape such as cassettes?	*Magnetism*
8		The science which studies the history of the Earth's crust is called what?	*Geology*
9		If a wheel has a circumference of 4 m, how many turns will it take to go 100 m?	*25*
10		How many Great Lakes are there in North America?	*Five*
11		The initials WWF are the short name of which international organization that protects animals?	*The World Wide Fund for Nature*
12		If someone asked you to send a hard copy, what would you need to do?	*Print out a computer file on to paper*
13		What do you call a piece of land that juts out when three of its four sides border water?	*A peninsula*
14		What parts of the body does an 'ENT' specialist treat?	*Ear, nose and throat*
15		Which part of the body does Alzheimer's disease affect?	*The brain*

Quiz 95
Question 1

Quiz 95
Question 13

Quiz 97 Level 3

Questions

Answers

		Question	Answer
1		On which continent would you find prairie dogs?	*North America*
2		What is a crevasse?	*A narrow gap in a glacier or rock face*
3		What important gas did Joseph Priestly discover in 1774?	*Oxygen*
4		What item of clothing shares its name with the process of starting up a computer?	*Boot*
5		What is the name of the projectile used in badminton?	*Shuttlecock*
6		What is a pot-hole?	*A cave that goes straight down*
7		If a person is short-sighted, do they have trouble seeing nearby objects or objects at a distance?	*Objects at a distance*
8		How many centimetres are there in an inch?	*2.54*
9		What part of a fan pushes the air?	*The blades*
10		Which three letters would a ship's radio operator send out as an emergency call?	*SOS*
11		Which bird of prey has New World and Old World varieties?	*Vultures*
12		Which is the largest continent?	*Asia*
13		What type of biologist studies the plants and animals of the seas?	*A marine biologist*
14		What is one-third squared?	*One-ninth*
15		Which planet is furthest from the Sun?	*Neptune*

Quiz 98
Question 9

Quiz 98
Question 8

Quiz 98 Level 3

Questions

Answers

#		Question	Answer
1		Do stars become red giants near the end of their lives or near the beginning?	*Near the end*
2		Where do musk oxen live?	*In the far north, in the Arctic region*
3		Which group of people take the Hippocratic Oath before they can begin their career?	*Doctors*
4		Which blood vessels take blood from the heart to the different parts of the body?	*Arteries*
5		What kind of reptile, famous for walking slowly, can live to be 150 years old?	*Tortoise*
6		Who invented the first battery?	*Alessandro Volta in 1800*
7		What type of thick woodland near the Equator is hot and humid all the time?	*A rainforest*
8		Which bird, native to New Zealand, shares its name with a fruit?	*Kiwi*
9		What do Americans call a spanner?	*A wrench*
10	$\sqrt{x}$	A kilogram is roughly 2.2 pounds. How many pounds are there in 15 kg?	*33*
11		Taste bud cells distinguish four basic flavours, sweet, sour, bitter and what?	*Salty*
12		What would a zoologist study?	*Animals*
13		Most cars have how many gears for going forward?	*Four or five*
14		A problem with which organ can cause people to lose their balance?	*The ear*
15		If a material is said to be ductile, what can be done to it?	*It can be drawn into thin wires*

Quiz 97
Question 5

Quiz 97
Question 4

Quiz 97
Question 9

Quiz 99 Level 3

Questions

Answers

		Questions	Answers
1		What is an elver?	*A young eel*
2		What do rivets join together?	*Pieces of metal*
3		The iris is part of which organ?	*The eye*
4		Which other Australian animal resembles a wallaby?	*Kangaroo*
5		What are the three common states of matter?	*Solid, liquid and gas*
6		Which type of climate receives more rainfall – semi-arid or temperate?	*Temperate*
7		Turbot, flounder and marlin are all examples of which type of animal?	*Fish*
8		Two knobs on a sound system adjust the pitch. One is the bass; what is the other?	*Treble*
9		What hard seed grows on a palm tree?	*Coconut*
10	$\sqrt{x}$	What type of circles are concentric?	*Those with the same centre*
11		What method of joining metals heats them until they melt and mix together?	*Welding*
12		The explorer Richard Peary became the first person to reach which place in 1909?	*The North Pole*
13	$\sqrt{x}$	A diagonal line drawn between two corners of a square produces which two shapes?	*Two right triangles*
14		Is there more dry land north or south of the Equator?	*North*
15		Which type of blood vessels take blood from differents part of the body back to the heart?	*Veins*

Quiz 100
Question 9

Quiz 100
Question 7

Quiz 100
Question 12

Quiz 100 Level 3

	Questions	Answers
1	Does a line of longitude run north-south or east-west across a map?	North-south
2	The Zeppelin built in 1900 was the first successful example of what kind of craft?	The first rigid controllable airship
3	What does a vacuum flask do to liquids?	Keeps them hot or cool
4	Eating too much of a fat called cholesterol can lead to what type of disease?	Heart disease
5	A hexagon has how many sides?	Six
6	Which is the smallest continent?	Australia
7	The optic nerves lead to the brain from where?	The eyes
8	What type of scientist would provide information about an occluded front?	A meteorologist (weather person)
9	If you are given one playing card, what is the probability of getting an ace?	1/13
10	What word describes the information used by a computer?	Data
11	Cirrus, cumulus and nimbus are all types of what?	Cloud
12	How many dominoes are in a standard set?	28
13	75% saltpetre, 15% charcoal and 10% sulphur make up which substance?	Gunpowder
14	What type of engineer would design and build roads, bridges and tunnels?	A civil engineer
15	How many grams are there in 2 kg?	2,000

Quiz 99
Question 9

Quiz 99
Question 7

Quiz 101 Level 3

Questions

Answers

#	Question	Answer
1	What term is used to describe a multiple birth of five children?	*Quintuplets*
2	Which sense do hedgehogs rely on to find their food?	*Smell*
3	Which is the smallest planet?	*Mercury*
4	What is a skink?	*A type of lizard*
5	Which of the following is a prime number: 12, 21, 31, 39, 49?	*31*
6	What has happened to a bone that is fractured?	*It has broken*
7	What occurs when the Moon lies in front of the Sun?	*A solar eclipse*
8	What type of doctor would operate on the cerebellum?	*A brain surgeon*
9	The piano is a percussion instrument: true or false?	*True*
10	On which planet did the Pathfinder mission land in 1966?	*Mars*
11	Bread mould is closely related to which important medicine?	*Penicillin*
12	What type of angle is described as being acute?	*One that is smaller than a right angle*
13	On a ship, what is the screw?	*The propeller*
14	The epidermis is the outer layer of what?	*The skin*
15	What kind of pink bird can grow up to 1.5 m tall?	*Flamingo*

Quiz 102
Question 3

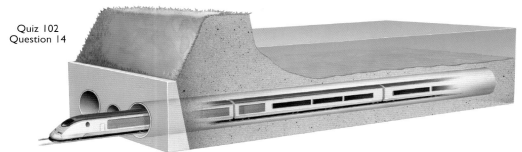

Quiz 102
Question 14

Quiz 102 Level 3

	Questions	Answers
1	What is the fruit of an oak tree called?	*An acorn*
2	What type of body tissue expands and relaxes in order to let people move?	*Muscle*
3	If a mathematician is using a protractor, what is she or he measuring?	*Angles*
4	What type of device throws the image of a film onto a screen?	*A projector*
5	What is the name of the large island that lies off the southeast coast of Africa?	*Madagascar*
6	Which grow to be longer – crocodiles or alligators?	*Crocodiles (the Asian and Australian type)*
7	What is produced by a solar cell?	*Electricity*
8	What metal is used to galvanise steel or iron?	*Zinc*
9	Complete the following: $\frac{4}{12} = \frac{6}{?}$	*18*
10	The range of colours that the human eye can detect is known as what?	*The visible spectrum*
11	Which river has two branches known as the White and the Blue?	*The Nile*
12	If a wheel turns two times, how many degrees has it travelled through?	*720*
13	If a disease is hereditary, how does someone catch it?	*It is inherited from one or both parents*
14	Which famous length of railway passes between Folkestone, England and Calais, France?	*The Channel Tunnel*
15	Centigrade is another name for which measurement?	*Celsius (temperature)*

Quiz 101
Question 7

Quiz 103 Level 3

Questions

Answers

		Question	Answer
1		What do you call a small piece of wood, glass or metal that gets stuck in the skin?	*A splinter*
2		How many inches are there in 15 feet?	*180*
3		Into which body of water does the Danube River empty?	*The Black Sea*
4		Does the average roomful of air weighs 15, 25, 35 or 45 kg?	*45 kg*
5		What small computer storage device was introduced in 1970?	*The floppy disk*
6		What do the letters DC stand for in electricity?	*Direct current*
7		Which group of mammals share their name with a kind of tooth?	*Canines*
8		What lens touches the cornea when worn?	*Contact lens*
9		Which word describes an inward-curving surface, like the inside of a bowl?	*Concave*
10		What do you call a small elevator that transports items between floors?	*A dumbwaiter*
11		Who are more likely to suffer from colour blindness – men or women?	*Men*
12		How many hours have you slept if you fell asleep at 2015 and woke at 0745?	*11 ½*
13		What radioactive element was discovered by the German Martin Klaproth in 1841?	*Uranium*
14		What do you call the spiral lines running down a screw?	*The thread*
15		Which fruit was once known as the Chinese gooseberry?	*The kiwi fruit*

Quiz 104
Question 14

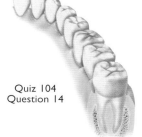

Quiz 104
Question 1

Quiz 104 Level 3

Questions
Answers

		Questions	Answers
1		Which is the odd one out: snail, beetle, turtle, crab?	*Turtle, it is the only one with a backbone*
2		What type of injury can be either first degree, second degree or third degree?	*Burn*
3		What is a monorail?	*A railway using one rail rather than two*
4		What do you call the longest side of a right-angled triangle?	*The hypotenuse*
5		Which river combines with the Mississippi to form one of the world's longest river systems?	*The Missouri*
6		What does a Geiger counter measure?	*Radiation (radioactivity)*
7		Where do aquatic plants live?	*In the water*
8		How many sides has a pentagon?	*Five*
9		What ape is most closely related to humans?	*Chimpanzees*
10		Galileo dropped objects from which famous building to learn about how fast things fall?	*The Leaning Tower of Pisa*
11		The Ural Mountains form part of the border between which two continents?	*Europe and Asia*
12		The word *algebra* comes from which language?	*Arabic*
13		Which substance makes fireworks explode?	*Gunpowder*
14		Enamel, the hardest substance in the body, is the outside covering of what?	*The teeth*
15		Which is the densest planet in our Solar System?	*Earth*

Quiz 103
Question 5

Quiz 103
Question 7

Quiz 103
Question 15

Quiz 105 Level 3

Questions | Answers

#	Question	Answer
1	What do you call an open sore on the lining of the intestine?	*An ulcer*
2	How many degrees has a quadrant?	*90 (it is one-quarter of a circle)*
3	What is sorghum?	*A grain grown in warm climates*
4	Which food grows in a 'paddy' field?	*Rice*
5	British scientist William Fox Talbot was a pioneer in which field?	*Photography*
6	What do you call a big ship or lorry that carries large amounts of liquid?	*A tanker*
7	What fruit grows in groups called 'hands'?	*Bananas*
8	In which country would you find 'Tornado Alley'?	*The United States*
9	What cords vibrate when we talk?	*Vocal cords*
10	What is a samoyed?	*A breed of dog*
11	Which word can be added to the following to make three tools: hack, band, jig?	*Saw*
12	What man-made objects orbit the Earth and help with communication?	*Satellites*
13	What is 90 percent of 90?	*81*
14	What colour flame is produced when a substance containing copper is burned?	*Bluish green*
15	Which uses more of the body's energy – swimming or tennis?	*Swimming*

Quiz 106
Question 6

Quiz 106
Question 15

Quiz 106 Level 3

Questions

Answers

#		Question	Answer
1		What is amnesia?	*Loss of memory*
2		What scale do scientists use to measure the severity of an earthquake?	*The Richter scale*
3		What proportion of the air is oxygen: one-fifth, one-eighth, or one-tenth?	*One-fifth*
4		What is 30 percent of 30?	*9*
5		What tool uses air and liquid to determine if something lies flat?	*A spirit level*
6		What kind of amphibian shares its name with a part of a horse's hoof?	*A frog*
7		What kind of test would an audiologist give?	*A hearing test*
8		Which British engineer is associated with the invention of the jet engine?	*Sir Frank Whittle*
9		A 'supernova' is the birth of a star. True or false?	*False – it is the death of a star*
10		In 1901, Hubert Cecil Booth patented and produced which household tool?	*The vacuum cleaner*
11		How many grams are there in a metric tonne?	*One million*
12		What connects the following names: O'Hare, Charles de Gaulle, Kennedy?	*They are names of major airports*
13		What type of animal lives in a sett?	*Badger*
14		Which two oceans meet at the Cape of Good Hope?	*Atlantic and Indian*
15		Which bodily organ's function does a dialysis machine replace?	*Kidney*

Quiz 105
Question 7

Quiz 105
Question 10

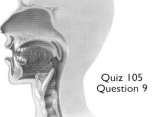

Quiz 105
Question 9

Quiz 107 Level 3

Questions

Answers

		Question	Answer
1		Which is larger – Mars or Saturn?	*Saturn*
2		In 1782 which French brothers made a flight in a hot air balloon?	*The Montgolfier brothers*
3		The 37 species of toucan all live in which continent?	*South America*
4		In which disease do some of the body's cells go out of control and multiply?	*Cancer*
5		Which type of metal is usually measured in carats?	*Gold*
6		What aid for sailors was built at Alexandria, Egypt?	*A lighthouse*
7		Which sleek sea animal has breeding grounds called rookeries?	*Seals*
8		Which line of tropic runs through South America, Africa and Australia?	*The Tropic of Capricorn*
9		If an engineer is measuring a moving object's RPMs, what is he or she checking?	*Revolutions per Minute*
10		What two muscles are used to lift the forearm?	*Bicep and tricep*
11		Which small weapon did Samuel Colt invent in 1835?	*The revolver*
12		A block and tackle is a group of what?	*Pulleys*
13		Which is larger, ¼ or ⁰⁄₁₆?	*Neither, they are both zero*
14		In which country is the famous volcano Mt Fuji?	*Japan*
15		Which shellfish produces pearls?	*Oyster*

Quiz 108
Question 9

Quiz 108 Level 3

Questions

Answers

		Questions	Answers
1		Who invented Morse Code in 1835?	*Samuel Morse*
2		What does exhalation mean?	*Breathing out*
3		What happens if you cube a number?	*You multiply it by itself twice*
4		What does a mycologist study?	*Fungi*
5		What do some animals do in order to survive the cold of winter?	*They hibernate*
6		Cape Horn is the southern tip of which continent?	*South America*
7		A midwife would be present at which important milestone in your life?	*Your birth*
8		Which cells in the human body do not have a nucleus?	*Red blood cells*
9		What bird is used in races because of its exceptional homing ability?	*Pigeon*
10		What are the two upper chambers of the heart called?	*The atria*
11		What is the name of the system used for satellite navigation?	*The Global Positioning System*
12		What can you tell from the rings of a tree trunk?	*The age of the tree*
13		How many minutes are there in a day?	*1,440*
14		Which planet is nearest the Earth?	*Mars*
15		Most lorries use what type of fuel?	*Diesel*

Quiz 107
Question 10

Quiz 107
Question 6

Quiz 109 Level 3

Questions

Answers

1		What do Americans call a tap?	*A faucet*
2		If a surgeon gave someone a pacemaker, what part of the body would it help?	*The heart*
3		What is a loom?	*A machine for weaving cloth*
4		What do you call an animal that can live on land or in the water?	*Amphibian*
5		Which type of tooth is used for grinding food?	*Molar*
6		How many sides has a polygon?	*3 or more (it's a many-sided figure)*
7		Which comet orbits the Sun every 76 years?	*Halley's comet*
8		What would a spider use its spinnerets for?	*Producing threads (used in webs)*
9		Which element has the chemical symbol Fe?	*Iron*
10		What is 150 percent of 12?	*18*
11		What process in humans starts with an ovum and ends with a fetus?	*Pregnancy*
12		Which is the odd one out: panther, cheetah, hyena, jaguar?	*Hyena (the others are all large cats)*
13		Which planet is the closest in size to Earth?	*Venus*
14		Which device measures the distance a vehicle has travelled?	*An odometer*
15		How does a python kill its prey?	*By crushing it*

Quiz 110
Question 10

Quiz 110
Question 6

Quiz 110
Question 3

Quiz 110 Level 3

	Questions	Answers
1	What type of instrument uses two or more lenses to make small objects appear much larger?	*Microscope*
2	A famous wrestling ring in the United States is named after a mathematical shape. What is it?	*The Octagon*
3	What in the body are the *rectus abdominus* and *deltoid* examples of?	*Muscles*
4	What type of medical professional performs root canal treatments?	*A dentist*
5	What is the chemical symbol of Zinc?	*Zn*
6	What name is given to the graphic recording of the electrical changes in the heart?	*ECG (electrocardiogram)*
7	Which raw material is most plastic made from?	*Oil*
8	What is the Earth's closest neighbour in space?	*The Moon*
9	What did Ladislao Biro invent in 1933?	*The ballpoint pen*
10	What kind of creature uses a 'trap-door' to catch its prey?	*A trap-door spider*
11	If an insect flaps its wings 30 times a second, how many times will it flap in 2 minutes?	*3,600*
12	What job does a clutch do on a car?	*It separates the gears*
13	What are your incisors?	*The flat front teeth*
14	What black and white creature is of the genus *Equus*?	*Zebra*
15	What machine can vary its density to travel underwater or on the water's surface?	*A submarine or submersible*

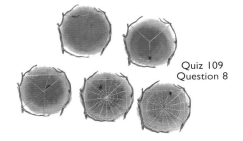

Quiz 109
Question 8

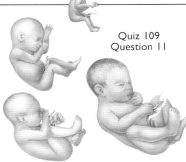

Quiz 109
Question 11

Quiz 111 Level 3

Questions

Answers

		Questions	Answers
1		Which mammal is the only one that can fly?	*A bat*
2		Which broadcast radio waveband operates from 160–225 kHz?	*Long wave*
3		What job does bile perform in the body?	*It helps digest food*
4		What type of insect makes huge mounds more than 2 m tall in Australia?	*Termites*
5		What does a botanist study?	*Plants*
6		Which is the world's largest desert?	*The Sahara*
7		A nonadecagon has how many sides?	*Nineteen*
8		Barbary apes live in only one small part of Europe. Where is it?	*Gibraltar*
9		In what year did a turbojet first successfully fly?	*1941*
10		What is the square root of 64?	*8*
11		If a doctor recommends taking insulin regularly, from which disease is the patient suffering?	*Diabetes*
12		About 95 percent of the body's calcium is found in which two areas?	*Teeth and bones*
13		Which instrument displays the change in electrical voltages over time?	*Oscilloscope*
14		What does the 'N' stand for on a car's gearshift?	*Neutral*
15		What was the name of the first space probe to send back pictures of Venus?	*Venera*

Quiz 112
Question 1

Quiz 112
Question 8

Quiz 112 Level 3

Questions | Answers

#		Question	Answer
1		What name is given to the fertilization of plants by animals?	*Animal pollination*
2		What happens to your heart rate as you grow older?	*It slows down*
3		How many metres are there in 5.5 km?	*5,500*
4		What do Americans call the boot of a car?	*The trunk*
5		What does a thermometer measure?	*Temperature*
6		Jupiter has the biggest moon in our Solar System. What is it called?	*Ganymede*
7		Urine is 95 percent water: true or false?	*True*
8		What kind of lizard, with a long tongue, is renowned for its colour-changing abilities?	*Chameleon*
9		Fireworks were invented by people living in which country?	*China*
10		Which vitamin, found in liver and green vegetables, helps with clotting blood?	*Vitamin K*
11		True or false: birds are the only animals with feathers?	*True*
12		Ancient scientists believed that there were only four elements: earth, fire, air and what else?	*Water*
13		What is 50% of 122?	*61*
14		What is nausea?	*The feeling that you need to be sick*
15		How big is one nanometre?	*One-billionth of a metre*

Quiz 111
Question 1

Quiz 111
Question 4

Quiz 113 Level 3

Questions

Answers

		Questions	Answers
1		What is the liquid part of blood called?	*Plasma*
2		Which is usually bigger – a gulf or a bay?	*A gulf*
3		In which war were the first jet planes used?	*The Second World War*
4		What does 'biodegradable' mean?	*Able to rot away naturally*
5		Which part of the body is affected by conjunctivitus?	*The eye*
6		What kind of paper is used to measure acids and alkalis?	*Litmus paper*
7		What ape shares its name with the inventor of the heart-lung machine?	*Gibbon*
8		How many decades are there in a millennium?	*100*
9		What is another name for a snowstorm?	*Blizzard*
10		Which is larger – a destroyer or a battleship?	*A battleship*
11		What are the names of the three segments of a bee?	*Head, thorax, abdomen*
12		Biology is the study of what?	*Living things*
13		Which term describes half of the diameter of a circle?	*The radius*
14		What type of food plant do Americans call eggplant?	*Aubergine*
15		What word describes a region's average weather over a long period of time?	*Its climate*

Quiz 114
Question 11

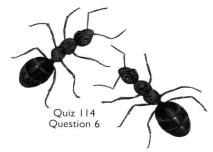

Quiz 114
Question 6

Quiz 114
Question 8

Quiz 114 Level 3

Questions

Answers

1		What type of rock is formed from cooled volcanic magma?	*Igneous*
2		What type of animal has kids?	*Goat*
3		Which two oceans does the Panama Canal connect?	*The Atlantic and Pacific*
4		If five musical octets were singing together, how many singers would be performing?	*40*
5		In which part of the body would you find grey matter?	*The brain and spinal column*
6		What kind of insect has red, army and honey varieties?	*Ants*
7		What type of disaster occurred at Chernobyl, Ukraine, in 1986?	*A nuclear reactor exploded*
8		In what type of landscape would you expect to find a chamois?	*Mountainside*
9		What fraction of a circle is a section measuring 270 degrees?	*Three-quarters*
10		What is the common name of the tibia?	*The shinbone*
11		What covers the majority of molluscs?	*A shell*
12		At room temperature, is helium a gas, a liquid or a solid?	*A gas*
13		A 'liner' is another word for what type of transport?	*Passenger ship*
14		What is the name of the light-sensitive lining behind the eye?	*The retina*
15		What do you call a large amount of snow and ice that tumbles quickly down a mountainside?	*An avalanche*

Quiz 113
Question 11

Quiz 113
Question 7

Quiz 115 Level 4

Questions | Answers

#	Question	Answer
1	What is the medical term for the voice box?	*The larynx*
2	What links the rhea, emu and dodo?	*They are flightless birds*
3	Which two planets have no known moons?	*Mercury and Venus*
4	What is 25 percent of one-quarter?	*One-sixteenth*
5	What does a seismologist study?	*Earthquakes*
6	Which colour is at the opposite end of the spectrum from red?	*Violet*
7	What does a sextant measure?	*The angle of the Sun against the horizon*
8	What are krill?	*Tiny sea animals resembling shrimp*
9	How many cuticles does a human have?	*20*
10	Pi is multiplied by the diameter of a circle to calculate what?	*Circumference*
11	Which is the odd one out – sedimentary, igneous and glabrous?	*Glabrous – the rest are types of rock*
12	What do you call someone who studies volcanoes?	*A vulcanologist*
13	What type of engine powers most cars?	*Internal combustion*
14	What is an atoll?	*A ring-shaped reef surrounding a lagoon*
15	What does 'avian' mean?	*Relating to birds*

Quiz 116
Question 3

Quiz 116
Question 11

Quiz 116
Question 4

Quiz 116 Level 4

Questions | Answers

#	Question	Answer
1	What is the aurora borealis?	*Northern lights*
2	What is the process that plants use to convert carbon dioxide and light into protein?	*Photosynthesis*
3	What does an anemometer measure?	*Wind speed*
4	Where in your body is the patella?	*Your leg (the kneecap)*
5	What is the square root of 441?	*21*
6	Who said 'Eureka' when he noticed that a body displaces an equal volume of water in a bath?	*Archimedes*
7	What type of plant is a perennial?	*One that grows year after year*
8	Reflector and refractor are types of what scientific instrument?	*Optical telescope*
9	Edwin 'Buzz' Aldrin was the second person to do what?	*Walk on the Moon*
10	Does ice weigh more or less than liquid water?	*Less*
11	What do we call the band of millions of rocks that orbit between Mars and Jupiter?	*The asteroid belt*
12	What do you do when you expectorate?	*Spit*
13	A fulcrum is an important part of what type of machine?	*A lever*
14	Which part of the body does osteoporosis affect?	*The bones*
15	If you added the four smallest prime numbers, what would the sum be?	*17 (2+3+5+7)*

Quiz 115
Question 3

Quiz 115
Question 2

Quiz 115
Question 15

Quiz 117 Level 4

Questions | Answers

#		Question	Answer
1		What is osteology the study of – bones, blood or internal organs?	*Bones*
2		Which system do submarines use to 'hear' underwater?	*Sonar*
3		When was Pluto officially classified as a dwarf planet?	*2006*
4		What type of animal travels in pods?	*Whales or dolphins*
5		What does AIDS stand for?	*Acquired Immune Deficiency Syndrome*
6		The Austrian monk Gregor Mendel is associated with which science?	*Genetics*
7		What sort of mineral has many flat faces and is symmetrical?	*A crystal*
8		What term describes a cloud of particles suspended in a gas?	*An aerosol*
9		What, in degrees, is the sum of the three angles of a triangle?	*180°*
10		Which gas forms about 78% of air?	*Nitrogen*
11		What is the scientific name for rusting?	*Oxidation*
12		'Air cushion vehicle' is another term for what means of transport?	*Hovercraft*
13		What is the continental shelf?	*Land that extends out into the ocean*
14		What word describes an animal or plant whose parents belong to two different species?	*A hybrid*
15		What is one-half cubed?	*One-eighth*

Quiz 118
Question 13

Quiz 118
Question 14

Quiz 118 Level 4

Questions

Answers

		Question	Answer
1		What is the process whereby yeast acts on sugar to produce alcohol and carbon dioxide?	*Fermentation*
2		Which is the world's smallest ocean?	*The Arctic Ocean*
3		Sir Alexander Fleming is associated chiefly with the development of which medicine?	*Penicillin*
4		Within ten, how many bones does an adult have in his or her body?	*206*
5		What type of instrument, 305 m across, is located in Arecibo, Puerto Rico?	*Radio telescope*
6		What are the troposphere, stratosphere and mesosphere?	*Layers of the Earth's atmosphere*
7		Which letter represents the speed of light in mathematical equations?	*C*
8		What was the name of the first spacecraft to leave the Solar System?	**Voyager 1**
9		Does an electron have a positive, negative or neutral charge?	*Negative*
10		How many inches are there in 12 feet?	*144*
11		What does an ornithologist study?	*Birds*
12		How do we describe the stream of electrically-charged particles sprayed from the Sun?	*Solar wind*
13		What kind of vehicle is Henry Ford famous for making?	*Car*
14		Charles Babbage is credited with designing the first what, in the 1830s?	*Computer*
15		What is the name of the winds that blow on either side of the Equator?	*Trade winds*

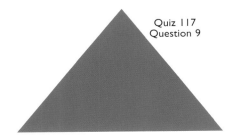

Quiz 117
Question 9

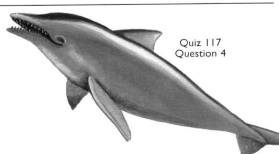

Quiz 117
Question 4

Quiz 119 Level 4

	Questions	Answers
1	Which famous oceanographer tested the first Aqualung in 1943?	*Jacques Cousteau*
2	What is measured by photometry?	*Light*
3	Using Roman numerals, what is XVI times L?	*DCCC*
4	What is a baby kangaroo called?	*A joey*
5	The Montgolfier brothers first rode in what type of transport in 1783?	*Hot-air balloon*
6	The word 'bit', used in computing, is formed from which two words?	*Binary digit*
7	What term describes a mixture of two or more metals?	*An alloy*
8	Tenochtitlan, capital city of the Aztecs, was built by people with no knowledge of which invention?	*The wheel*
9	What is another word for the arithmetic mean?	*Average*
10	What do we call the time that a baby spends inside its mother's womb?	*Gestation period or pregnancy*
11	Which planet is sometimes further from the Sun than dwarf planet Pluto?	*Neptune*
12	What is the name of the calculating device that has wooden balls sliding across wires?	*Abacus*
13	How many different blood groups are there among humans?	*Four*
14	Which type of cloud forms highest in the sky?	*Cirrus*
15	What do scientists call a collapsed star that is so massive that not even light can escape from it?	*A black hole*

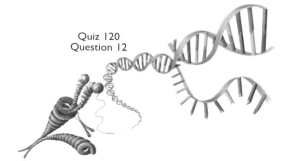

Quiz 120
Question 12

Quiz 120
Question 11

Quiz 120 Level 4

Questions

Answers

#		Question	Answer
1		What type of surgical operation takes a small amount of tissue and examines it for cancer?	*Biopsy*
2		Which chemical colours most plants green?	*Chlorophyll*
3		Which letter is to the right of 'S' on a computer keyboard?	*'D'*
4		What is the name of the Sun's atmosphere, which we can only see during a total eclipse?	*The corona*
5		What word describes the two days each year when night and day are exactly the same length?	*Equinox*
6		What term describes something that speeds up a chemical reaction between two other substances?	*A catalyst*
7		In which book did Charles Darwin publish his theory of evolution in 1859?	**On the Origin of Species**
8		If a clock displaying only numbers is digital, what word describes a clock with hands?	*Analogue*
9		What distinguishes marsupials from most other mammals?	***They have pouches to carry their young***
10		0.166666... is a decimal equivalent of which fraction?	*One-sixth*
11		Which planet has a Great Red Spot which is larger than Earth?	*Jupiter*
12		James Watson and Francis Crick discovered the structure of which substance?	*DNA*
13		Roughly how far away is a storm if you hear thunder ten seconds after a flash of lightning?	*3 km*
14		The eustachian tube links the throat to which organ?	*The ear*
15		Marie Curie, winner of Nobel Prizes for both Physics and Chemistry, was born where?	*Poland*

Quiz 119
Question 15

Quiz 119
Question 4

Quiz 121 Level 4

	Questions	Answers

1. What is the average age of a group of children aged 13, 12, 10, 6 and 4? — *9*

2. What is an apiarist? — *A beekeeper*

3. Coal is made up mostly of which non-metallic element? — *Carbon*

4. Which manufacturer established the first assembly line to produce his vehicles? — *Henry Ford*

5. What name is given to a frequency that is greater than that which can be heard by the human ear? — *Ultrasound*

6. Gabriel Fahrenheit, inventor of a widely used temperature scale, came from which country? — *Germany*

7. Which planet has two moons, named Deimos and Phobos? — *Mars*

8. How much is 35% of 300? — *105*

9. What do you call a cross between a horse and a donkey? — *A mule*

10. If a person is myopic, from what condition does he or she suffer? — *Near-sightedness*

11. What is five dozen divided by a score? — *Three*

12. What do electrical transformers do in relation to overall power supply? — *Reduce voltage*

13. Dendrochronology is a method of dating past events by looking at what? — *Tree rings*

14. To the nearest 50 million years, how long does it take the Sun to move around our galaxy? — *200 million years*

15. What is the word 'fax' short for? — *Facsimile transmission*

Quiz 122
Question 4

Quiz 122 Level 4

Questions

Answers

		Questions	Answers
1		Who invented the steam engine?	*Thomas Savery*
2		What term describes the air resistance that slows down aircraft?	*Drag*
3		Reduce $^{21}/_{39}$ to its simplest terms.	$^7/_{13}$
4		Zoology, a biological science, is the study of what?	*Animals*
5		Which type of coal is harder – bituminous or anthracite?	*Anthracite*
6		What do we call the process of shaping metal by hammering it while it is still hot?	*Forging*
7		Who invented the lightning rod?	*Benjamin Franklin*
8		Inhaled corticosteroids are the standard long-term treatment for what common disease?	*Asthma*
9		Which is the odd one out: apple, tomato, pea pod, potato?	*Potato (the others are all fruit)*
10		Who first observed the moons of Jupiter?	*Galileo Galilei*
11		What do you call the bursts of hot gas that occur during storms on the surface of the Sun?	*Solar flares*
12		A person runs 3 km a day to keep fit. How far will she run in total in May and June?	*183 km*
13		Which inventor described his work as "1 percent inspiration and 99 percent perspiration"?	*Thomas Edison*
14		Where in your body is the septum?	*Your nose*
15		Which was earlier – the Triassic or Jurassic Period?	*Triassic*

Quiz 121
Question 13

Quiz 121
Question 7

Quiz 121
Question 2

Quiz 123 Level 4

Questions

Answers

		Question	Answer
1		Joules and calories are measurements of what?	*Energy*
2		What does it mean if a satellite is described as having a geostationary orbit?	*It remains over the same point on Earth*
3		What is the name for the tissue that connects bones?	*Ligaments*
4		A Maglev train travels by using what type of technology?	*Magnetic levitation*
5		What term describes a three-dimensional photograph?	*A hologram*
6		Which common fraction is equivalent to 37.5 percent?	*⅜*
7		What does an audiologist study?	*Human hearing*
8		What kind of rocks are formed by material being deposited and compressed?	*Sedimentary rocks*
9		What is the LCD of a calculator?	*Liquid Crystal Display*
10		The word 'Mach', used in measuring speed, refers to what?	*The speed of sound in the air*
11		What is the job of the kidneys?	*To remove waste from the blood*
12		What would you have straightened if you visited an orthodontist?	*Your teeth*
13		How does the ozone layer protect us?	*By filtering out solar radiation*
14		Which is the body's largest gland?	*The liver*
15		Multiply 32 by the product of 2 and 4.	*256*

Quiz 124
Question 3

Quiz 124
Question 1

Quiz 124
Question 2

Quiz 124 Level 4

Questions

Answers

		Question	Answer
1		A banana is a type of berry: true or false?	*True*
2		Where would you find the Sea of Tranquillity?	*The Moon*
3		Which astronomer discovered Uranus?	*William Herschel*
4		What does vitamin D help keep strong and healthy?	*Bones and teeth*
5		What nationality was the famous mathematician Pythagoras?	*Greek*
6		What purpose does cartilage serve?	*It cushions bones*
7		The ancient measurement of the cubit was the length between which two parts of the body?	*Elbow and fingertip*
8		What do radio telescopes detect?	*Radiation given out by stars*
9		The word 'alluvial' refers to what?	*Soil deposited by flowing water*
10		Albert Sabin developed an oral (taken through the mouth) vaccine for which disease?	*Polio*
11		What was the name of the first manned spacecraft to land on the Moon?	*The Eagle*
12		Which part of the body is affected by otitis?	*The ear*
13		How many stars are estimated to be in the Milky Way: 20 billion, 200 million or 200 billion?	*200 billion*
14		At which temperature are Fahrenheit and Celsius readings the same?	*-40 degrees*
15		A gerontologist is a specialist in which area?	*The study of the elderly*

Quiz 123
Question 11

Quiz 123
Question 3

Quiz 125 Level 4

Questions

Answers

		Question	Answer
1		What do scientists call the temperature -273.15°C?	*Absolute zero*
2		What was the name of the astronomer who in 100 BC made the first catalogue of the stars?	*Hipparchus*
3		What is the common name for an integrated circuit?	*Microchip*
4		A rectangular garden has a perimeter of 40 m. If the garden is 8 m wide, how long is it?	*12 m*
5		Which planets are not visible to the naked eye?	*Uranus and Neptune*
6		Anton van Leeuwenhoek was credited with developing the first what?	*Microscope*
7		Which metallic elements are most common in meteorites?	*Iron and nickel*
8		Divide two gross by a dozen.	*24*
9		What is the medical name for the hip bone?	*The pelvis*
10		Which type of computer problem has the same name as a harmful biological agent?	*Virus*
11		Which gas is sometimes referred to as 'marsh gas'?	*Methane*
12		In the original metric system, a metre was defined as a ten-millionth of the distance between what?	*The North Pole and the Equator*
13		Where on your body would you find the metatarsal bone?	*The foot*
14		Which means of communication did Samuel Morse invent in the 1830s?	*The telegraph*
15		What is the square of half a dozen?	*36*

Quiz 126
Question 14

Quiz 126
Question 4

Quiz 126 Level 4

	Questions	Answers
1	To the nearest whole number, how many times weaker is the Moon's gravity than the Earth's?	*Six*
2	Write this number in figures: nine and three-quarter million.	*9,750,000*
3	Sir Isaac Newton defined what as an object's mass multiplied by its velocity?	*Its momentum*
4	In order to straighten your arm you must contract which muscle?	*The triceps*
5	What is the process that kills disease-producing micro-organisms in food and drink by heat?	*Pasteurisation*
6	A neurologist specializes in which area of science?	*The human nervous system*
7	The ten tallest mountains on Earth are all part of which range?	*The Himalayas*
8	What process converts petroleum, or crude oil, into usable fuels?	*Refining*
9	A lighthouse beam flashes every 12 seconds. How many times will it flash in a day?	*7,200*
10	George Eastman was an American inventor who developed flexible rolls of what material?	*Camera film*
11	A gorilla has prehensile toes. What does 'prehensile' mean?	*Able to grasp objects*
12	Which planet was discovered in 1846?	*Neptune*
13	What part of the body secretes the hormone insulin?	*The pancreas*
14	What is the common name for grape sugar?	*Glucose*
15	How many days are there in the first four months of a leap year?	*121*

Quiz 125
Question 9

Quiz 125
Question 5

Quiz 127 Level 4

Questions

Answers

1	In a class of 36 children there are 4 more boys than girls. How many girls are there?	*16*
2	What term do astronomers use to describe double, or twin stars?	*Binary stars*
3	What sort of medical operation reshapes parts of the body?	*Plastic surgery*
4	Which popular mp3 player was introduced in 2001?	*iPod*
5	What must be added to 73 mm to make a metre?	*927 mm*
6	What term describes the poisonous substance made by some snakes and scorpions?	*Venom*
7	James Watt gave his name to a measurement of what, as seen on light bulbs?	*Heat*
8	Is the Earth wider around the poles or around the Equator?	*The Equator*
9	What kitchen item is also a type of drum?	*Kettle*
10	Is the stigma on the male or female part of a flower?	*Female*
11	Where would you find the cerebellum?	*In the brain*
12	What is unusual about the star *Proxima Centauri*?	*It is the closest star to our Sun*
13	What is frozen dew?	*Frost*
14	How many seconds are there in three hours?	*10,800*
15	What is the fastest-moving planet in our Solar System?	*Mercury*

Quiz 128
Question 9

Quiz 128
Question 12

Quiz 128 Level 4

Questions

Answers

		Questions	Answers
1		According to the Greek astronomer Ptolemy, what was at the centre of the universe?	*The Earth*
2	$\sqrt{x}$	How long will it take a car, being driven at 80 km/h, to drive 720 km?	*9 hours*
3		Acrophobia is an intense fear of what?	*Heights*
4		In which century were the first ticking clocks invented?	*1300s*
5		Where in your body is the fibula?	*Your leg (shin bone)*
6		How long is a year on Saturn: 9, 29 or 79 years?	*29*
7		Which scientist famously said "God does not play dice"?	*Albert Einstein*
8	$\sqrt{x}$	If 5 kg of meat is used in a stew feeding 25 Scouts, how much meat does each Scout get?	*200 g*
9		What process distorts light so that a straw in a glass seems to be bent?	*Refraction*
10		Robert Goddard was the scientist who developed which type of vehicle?	*Liquid-fuelled rocket*
11		What do we call an automatic response by a muscle that does not involve thinking?	*A reflex*
12		*Sputnik 1* was launched into space by which country?	*Russia*
13		What makes Dolly the sheep so special?	*It was the first mammal to be cloned*
14	$\sqrt{x}$	How many hours are there in a fortnight?	*336*
15		Sodium chloride is the chemical name for which common substance?	*Table salt*

Quiz 127
Question 9

Quiz 127
Question 4

Quiz 127
Question 6

Quiz 129 Level 4

Questions

Answers

#	Question	Answer
1	What do fungi produce instead of seeds in order to reproduce?	*Spores*
2	A milkman delivers 40 litres of milk a day. How much will he deliver in August?	*1,240 litres*
3	Which planet has wind speeds that reach around 1,300 km/h?	*Saturn*
4	Who invented dynamite and gave his name to a famous series of prizes?	*Alfred Nobel*
5	Which feature of the human body is marked by loops and whorls?	*Fingertips*
6	What is a cosmonaut?	*It is the Russian term for astronaut*
7	Does sound travel faster or more slowly in water, compared with air?	*Faster*
8	A boy walks at 5 km/h. If he leaves at 1:30p.m. what time is it when he has travelled 30 km?	*7.30 p.m.*
9	Complete this sequence: 4, 8, 14, 22, ?	*32*
10	The leatherjacket is an insect more commonly given what name?	*Crane fly*
11	The clavicle is the medical term for which bone?	*The collarbone*
12	What is unusual about the star *Sirius*?	*It is the brightest in the sky*
13	What was the name of the Russian manned space station, launched in 1986?	*Mir*
14	What is the value of the 8 in 782,443?	*80,000*
15	What does an agronomist study?	*Management of the soil and crops*

Quiz 130
Question 3

Quiz 130
Question 11

Quiz 130 Level 4

Questions

Answers

		Questions	Answers
1		Which type of star is the hottest?	*Blue star*
2		What holds a balloon against a wall after you rub it against a woollen sweater?	*Static electricity*
3		In 1813, George Stephenson built the first successful what?	*Steam locomotive*
4		What type of vehicle uses ballast tanks?	*Submarine*
5		What percentage of twelve and a half litres is two and a half litres?	*20 percent*
6		Where in your body would you find villi?	*The stomach*
7		The Bay of Fundy in eastern Canada holds the record for which natural event?	*It has the highest rise and fall of tides*
8		What is humus?	*Decaying organic matter in the soil*
9		The word renal refers to which human organ?	*The kidney*
10		In computing, what do the letters VDU stand for?	*Visual Display Unit*
11		Who invented the telephone?	*Alexander Graham Bell*
12		If the base of a triangle is 3 cm and its height 4 cm, what is its area?	*6 cm squared*
13		Glucose, sucrose and fructose are examples of what?	*Sugars*
14		What are polar easterlies and Equator doldrums?	*Types of winds*
15		In 1975, two US spacecraft (named *Viking*) landed on which planet?	*Mars*

Quiz 129
Question 8

Quiz 129
Question 10

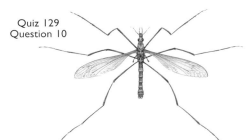

Quiz 129
Question 5

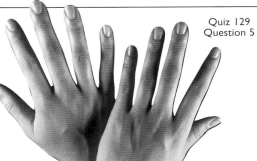

Quiz 131 Level 4

Questions

Answers

		Questions	Answers
1		How many people can the US space shuttle carry?	*Seven*
2		Apart from 0 and 1, list the set of squares of whole numbers up to 50.	*4, 9, 16, 25, 36, 49*
3		What does a hummingbird suck from a flower with its long beak?	*Nectar*
4		What can be total, partial or lunar?	*Eclipses*
5		What colour flame is produced when a substance containing potassium is burned?	*Purple*
6		How many people have stood on the Moon?	*11*
7		What percentage of 200 is 50?	*25 percent*
8		Which metric unit of area is just under 2.5 acres?	*Hectare*
9		What is the name for a tornado that occurs over the sea or a lake?	*Waterspout*
10		What is the name of the orbiting space telescope, launched in 1990?	*The Hubble Space Telescope*
11		What two metals make the alloy bronze?	*Copper and tin*
12		Which layer of a tree trunk contains the tubes that carry water and nutrients?	*The bark*
13		Where would you find canines and incisors?	*Your jaw (they are teeth)*
14		Which is the only even number that is also a prime number?	*2*
15		Some cameras are called SLR cameras. What do these letters stand for?	*Single Lens Reflex*

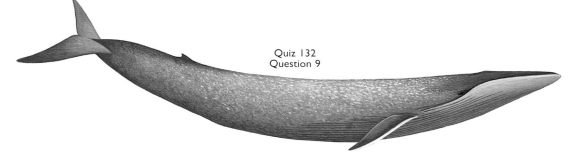

Quiz 132
Question 9

Quiz 132 Level 4

Questions

Answers

1	Who was the first person to use a telescope to study space?	*Galileo Galilei*
2	Which planet is between Saturn and Neptune?	*Uranus*
3	A square has an area of 36 square metres. What is its perimeter?	*24 metres*
4	What is a Chinook?	*A kind of helicopter*
5	An inch contains 25.4 of which unit of metric measurement?	*Millimetre*
6	What is the boiling point of water in Fahrenheit?	*212 degrees*
7	Where in your body would you find the humerus?	*Arm (upper arm bone)*
8	Which gas is used to fill toy balloons?	*Helium*
9	Which is the world's largest animal?	*The blue whale*
10	How many threes are in 39?	*13*
11	What do you call the clouds of space-dust in which new stars and planets form?	*Nebulae*
12	What type of object can be either reflecting, refracting or radio?	*Telescope*
13	Where would you find the cuticle?	*At the base of a fingernail or toenail*
14	Which scientist wrote a paper on 'Brownian motion' in 1956?	*Albert Einstein*
15	A car travels 11 km on each litre of petrol. How far will it go on 32 litres?	*352 km*

Quiz 131
Question 4

Quiz 131
Question 3

Quiz **133** Level **4**

	Questions	Answers
1	Which has the faster winds – a hurricane or a tornado?	*A tornado*
2	What is the common name for an adult's third molars?	*Wisdom teeth*
3	What is defined as the path an object follows as it moves through air under force?	*Trajectory*
4	What is the perimeter of a field 750 m long and 250 m wide?	*2000 m or 2 km*
5	The A&E department of a hospital deals with what type of cases?	*Accidents and Emergencies*
6	How many cells does an amoeba have?	*One*
7	Gunpowder was first developed in which country?	*China*
8	What part of the body protects the heart and lungs?	*Ribcage*
9	Four sacks of salt weigh 150 kg. What will a dozen sacks weigh?	*450 kg*
10	The American buffalo is really what type of animal?	*Bison*
11	Of all the planets in the Solar System, which one has the hottest surface?	*Venus*
12	What type of scientist would study quarks?	*Physicist (they are subatomic particles)*
13	An animal called a tsetse passes on diseases to humans and animals. What type of animal is it?	*A fly*
14	Composite, cinder cone and shield are the three main types of what?	*Volcano*
15	If M + 11 = 38, what does M equal?	*27*

Quiz 134
Question 6

Quiz 134
Question 4

Quiz 134 Level 4

Questions	Answers

Questions   **Answers**

1   In what part of the body would you find the renal medulla?   *The kidneys*

2   What is three thousand divided by five?   *Six hundred*

3   Where on a boat is its keel?   *On the bottom*

Quiz 133
Question 13

4   The okapi is the only living relative of which African animal?   *Giraffe*

5   What is 14 squared?   *196*

6   What is an obstetrician?   *Someone skilled in midwifery*

7   What does it mean when we say a star implodes?   *It collapses in on itself*

8   Where would you find the patella bone in your body?   *In the kneecap*

9   What is the total of three dozen, four score and two gross?   *404*

10   The highest mountain outside of Asia is on which continent?   *South America*

11   Which word describes trees that lose their leaves every year?   *Deciduous*

12   Paul Allen was the partner of which highly successful computer software developer?   *Bill Gates*

13   What device did Robert Watson-Watt invent in 1935?   *Radar*

14   Which muscle below the ribcage controls our breathing?   *The diaphragm*

15   What is the main ingredient used in making glass?   *Sand*

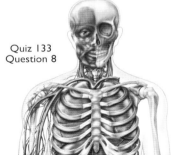

Quiz 133
Question 8

Quiz 133
Question 10

Quiz 135 Level 4

Questions

Answers

		Questions	Answers
1		A group of which type of animal is called a gaggle?	*Geese*
2		Where would you find a ridge of earth known as a moraine?	*By a glacier*
3		Two-thirds of the world's electricity power stations use which type of fuel?	*Coal*
4		Which type of bird has traditionally been used to carry written messages?	*Pigeon*
5		In base two numbers, what do you get by adding 11 and 1?	*100*
6		Does a star implode or explode to become a black hole?	*Implode*
7		What is the unit of electrical current called?	*The ampere (or amp)*
8		What do we call soil that remains frozen and never thaws?	*Permafrost*
9		A rocket takes 3 days to travel 384,000 km to the Moon. How many km/h is it travelling on average?	*5,333 km/h*
10		What did Igor Sikorsky do in 1939?	**Built the world's first helicopter**
11		If a doctor specializes in neo-natal care, who are his or her patients?	*Small babies*
12		What is a tarn?	*A mountain lake*
13		What, in terms of cinema, does the abbreviation SFX mean?	*Special effects*
14		In which ocean is the Humboldt Current?	*Pacific*
15		What is 0.7 of 90 kilometres?	*63 kilometres*

Quiz 136
Question 12

Quiz 136
Question 1

Quiz 136 Level 4

Questions

Answers

		Questions	Answers
1		Adelie, Emperor and King are all species of which animal?	*Penguin*
2		Beam, cantilever and suspension are all examples of what type of structure?	*Bridge*
3		By what name is the constellation Crux better known?	*The Southern Cross*
4		How many hours is 0.75 of a day?	*18 hours*
5		What is an ovum?	*An egg cell*
6		Robert Oppenheimer was an American physicist who helped develop which weapon?	*The atomic bomb*
7		What is the name of the process whereby a gas or vapour forms a liquid when it cools?	*Condensation*
8		In which ocean is the Sargasso Sea?	*Atlantic*
9		What links the following animals: passenger pigeon, Tasmanian tiger and dodo?	*They are all extinct*
10		An 800 ml milk bottle is 75% full. How much milk does it contain?	*600 ml*
11		Where on your body is the scapula?	*Shoulder (shoulder bone)*
12		What kind of frying is a chip pan used for?	*Deep-fat frying*
13		A petrologist studies what?	*Rocks*
14		Which two metals are combined to make brass?	*Copper and zinc*
15		Who was the first woman in space?	*Valentina Tereshkova*

Quiz 135
Question 4

Quiz 135
Question 1

Quiz 137 Level 4

Questions

Answers

		Question	Answer
1		What type of space instrument was named after Edwin Hubble?	*A telescope*
2		What is measured by the unit known as the coloumb?	*Electric charge*
3		What fraction of a circle is 120 degrees?	*One-third*
4		Where in the body is the cochlea?	*The ear (a liquid-filled tube)*
5		Gobi, Sonoran and Namib are all examples of what?	*Desert*
6		What is measured in millibars?	*Atmospheric pressure*
7		What were daguerreotypes?	*Early types of photographs*
8		Where would you find the stapedius muscle?	*The ear*
9		On which type of device might you find a resistor, capacitor, diode and transistor?	*A circuit board*
10		What is the ohm a measurement of?	*Electrical resistance*
11		How many weeks are there in three years?	*156*
12		What has happened to something that is dehydrated?	*Water has been removed from it*
13		What sort of a vehicle did Christopher Cockerell invent?	*The hovercraft*
14		What we normally call Arabic numerals were actually developed where?	*India*
15		When we sleep we pass through the REM cycle. What do the letters REM stand for?	*Rapid Eye Movement*

Quiz 138
Question 11

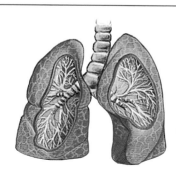

Quiz 138
Question 12

Quiz 138 Level 4

Questions

Answers

		Questions	Answers
1		What grows out of follicles?	*Hair*
2	$\sqrt{x}$	One-quarter of a number is 117. What is that number?	*468*
3		The expensive food known as caviar consists of the eggs of which fish?	*Sturgeon*
4		What do you call a boat with two hulls?	*A catamaran*
5		The atom was split by Ernest Walton and John Cockroft in what year?	*1932*
6		Is the wavelength of ultraviolet light longer or shorter than that of visible light?	*Shorter*
7		What is the name of the first sheep to be cloned?	*Dolly*
8		Which hereditary disease prevents blood from clotting properly?	*Haemophilia*
9		The Zodiac sign of the Archer is known as what?	*Sagittarius*
10		When did people first work with iron?	*About 1500 BC*
11		What does a cartographer do?	*Makes maps*
12		The word 'pulmonary' refers to which part of the body?	*The lungs*
13		Which is the largest island in the world?	*Greenland*
14	$\sqrt{x}$	A shopkeeper sold 72 cakes from his stock of 96. What percentage did he sell?	*75 percent*
15		What is kaolin an alternative name for?	*China clay*

Quiz 137
Question 4

Quiz 137
Question 13

Quiz 139 Level 4

Questions

Answers

		Questions	Answers
1		The Cambrian Period in geological history takes its name from discoveries in which country?	*Wales*
2		Which type of boat has underwater wings attached to the front and rear of its hull?	*A hydrofoil*
3		What does the diameter of a circle multiplied by pi equal?	*The circumference of the circle*
4		The duck-billed platypus and the spiny anteater are the only two mammals that do what?	*Lay eggs*
5		Guglielmo Marconi is associated with the development of what type of communication?	*Wireless telegraphy*
6		The Galapagos Islands are off the western coast of which continent?	*South America*
7		What kind of vehicle is a bathyscaphe?	*A submarine*
8		Where in the body is the tympanum?	*The ear (the eardrum)*
9		Which is the only metallic element that is liquid at room temperature?	*Mercury*
10		How many seconds are there in a week?	*604,800*
11		Hydraulics is the study of how which substances behave?	*Fluids*
12		What does antifreeze do to water's freezing point?	*It lowers it*
13		What links the following: Fuji, Mount St Helens and Mount Pelee?	*They are all active volcanoes*
14		How many minutes are there between 1107 hours and 1302 hours?	*115*
15		What is papyrus, used by the ancient Egyptians as a writing surface?	*A type of reed*

Quiz 140
Question 12

Quiz 140
Question 9

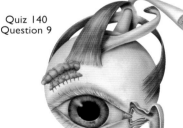
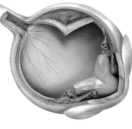

Quiz 140 Level 4

Questions

Answers

1		What is the lowest point below sea level on Earth?	*The Dead Sea*
2		In 1864, who discovered pasteurization as a method of killing germs?	*Louis Pasteur*
3		What is the fastest speed that anything can travel?	*The speed of light*
4		How many sides does an icosagon have?	*20*
5		What links the following: Ob, Orinoco, Okavango and Oder?	*They are all rivers*
6		What is another word for the cranium?	*The skull*
7		What is unusual about plants that are grown hydroponically?	*There is no soil*
8		To within 100 years, when was paper invented?	*AD 105*
9		Optometrists, ophthamologists and opticians are all concerned with what?	*Eyes (and vision)*
10		If the length of a rectangle is three times its 5 cm width, what is its perimeter?	*40 cm*
11		Which word is used to describe anything relating to breathing?	*Respiratory*
12		What type of animal is a sidewinder?	*A snake*
13		The Manhattan Project was a secret operation to develop what during World War II?	*The atomic bomb*
14		Which vitamin helps fight disease and helps seeing in the dark?	*Vitamin A*
15		Without using paper or a calculator, add together eighty-seven and fifty-three.	*140*

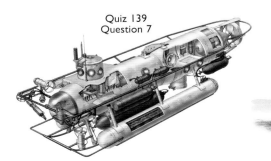

Quiz 139
Question 7

Quiz 139
Question 2

Quiz 141 Level 4

Questions

Answers

1	Which is the fastest land animal?	*The cheetah*
2	How many multiples of 3 are there below 20?	*Six (3, 6, 9, 12, 15, 18)*
3	In which mountain range would you find K2?	*Himalayas*
4	The word 'cardiac' refers to which part of the body?	*The heart*
5	What part of an atom did Ernest Rutherford discover in 1919?	*Proton*
6	Llamas and alpacas of South America are related to which animals of Africa and Asia?	*Camels*
7	What is the main source of raw material for plastic?	*Petroleum*
8	Human beings are bipeds. What does that mean?	*We walk on two legs*
9	What percentage of one hour and 20 minutes is 16 minutes?	*20 percent*
10	What do you call a small, dense star formed when a big star collapses under its own gravity?	*A neutron star*
11	If a technician adjusts levels of toner, what item of office equipment would he or she be mending?	*Photocopier*
12	What is latex?	*The liquid sap of the rubber tree*
13	Which American inventor counts electric light and sound recording amongst his inventions?	*Thomas Alva Edison*
14	Which skin ailment is commonly found among people who suffer from asthma?	*Eczema*
15	Uluru is the Aboriginal name for which huge rock outcrop in Australia?	*Ayers Rock*

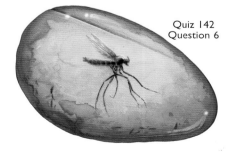

Quiz 142
Question 6

Quiz 142
Question 4

Quiz 142 Level 4

Questions

Answers

		Questions	Answers
1		By what name is the Pleiades constellation commonly known?	*The Seven Sisters*
2		What happens to time as something approaches the speed of light?	*It slows down*
3		Which published mathematician also won critical acclaim as a children's writer?	*Lewis Carroll*
4		What kind of waves are used in a remote control?	*Infra-red*
5		What is the name of the sharp knife used by surgeons during operations?	*Scalpel*
6		What is amber?	*The fossilized sap of conifers*
7		Where is the Ross Ice Shelf?	*Antarctica*
8		What is the square root of 225?	*15*
9		Roald Amundsen was the first person to reach which place on Earth?	*The South Pole*
10		Which explosive gas was once used to inflate airships?	*Hydrogen*
11		What does AC stand for in electrical matters?	*Alternating current*
12		What do we call the boundary between two air masses?	*A front*
13		How many degrees Fahrenheit is 10 degrees Celsius?	*50 degrees*
14		A train travels at 140 km/h. How far would it travel in 2 hours and 15 minutes?	*315 km*
15		What does a chronometer measure?	*Time*

Quiz 141
Question 1

Quiz 141
Question 6

Quiz 143 Level 4

Questions

Answers

		Questions	Answers
1		What is an archipelago?	*A group of islands*
2		How many degrees is half a semicircle?	*90 degrees*
3		What is a biplane? Quiz 144 Question 13	*A plane with two sets of wings*
4		Johann Kepler was the first to argue that planets do not travel in circles, but in which shape?	*Ellipses*
5		Ayrshire, Hereford and Friesian are breeds of which animal?	*Cattle*
6		Where is Arnhem Land?	*Australia*
7		Which system of communications uses flags to represent letters and words?	*Semaphore*
8		In which field of study were Sigmund Freud and Carl Jung pioneers?	*Psychiatry*
9		A shop sold 87,000 ml of orange juice from a total stock of 100 litres. How many litres were left?	*13 litres*
10		What kind of beam is used to read barcodes?	*Laser*
11		What is the biggest group of amphibians with more than 3,400 species?	*Frogs and toads*
12		What are loose rocks and stones on the side of a mountain called?	*Scree*
13		What is the Chinese system of medical treatment that uses needles in the body?	*Acupuncture*
14		Pigs sometimes help farmers sniff out which valuable underground fungi?	*Truffles*
15		Humphrey Davy invented a safety lamp for use in which industry?	*Mining*

Quiz 144
Question 14

Quiz 144 Level 4

Questions

Answers

		Question	Answer
1		Divide the product of a pair and three score by half a dozen.	*20*
2		How is the mineral pyrite sometimes known?	*Fool's gold*
3		How many faces has a dodecahedron?	*12*
4		The Sandwich Islands was the former name for which group of islands in the Pacific?	*Hawaii*
5		What does the Heimlich Manoeuvre, used in first aid, aim to do?	*Clear a blocked air passage*
6		How many hours are there in October?	*745 (the clocks go back one hour!)*
7		If a doctor prescribed tablets for a migraine, what type of ailment would he or she be treating?	*A severe headache*
8		Which great waterway opened in 1914?	*The Panama Canal*
9		What is phobophobia?	*Fear of being afraid*
10		An electrocardiagram (ECG) indicates electrical activity in which organ?	*The heart*
11		Athlete's foot is an infection by what substance?	*Fungus*
12		Pollenosis is the common name for what complaint?	*Hay fever*
13		What measuring device shares its name with a part of a fish?	*Scales*
14		The Gatling Gun was an early version of which weapon?	*Machine gun*
15		In a bicycle race a man covers 30 km in 40 minutes. What is his speed in km/h?	*45 km/h*

Quiz 143
Question 5

Quiz 143
Question 3

Quiz 145 Level 4

Questions   Answers

#	Question	Answer
1	What is the name for a mixture of falling rain and melting snow?	*Sleet*
2	In which country could you ride on the Bullet Train?	*Japan*
3	Which bird is associated with wisdom?	*The owl*
4	Which are the prime numbers in this list: 17, 46, 61, 78, 93?	*17 and 61*
5	Which highly infectious illness is caused by the varicella zoster virus?	*Chicken pox*
6	What does 'aft' mean on a ship or boat?	*To the rear*
7	Ascorbic acid is another name for which vitamin?	*Vitamin C*
8	What is the largest cruise liner currently in operation?	**Queen Mary II**
9	What record does Robert Wadlow hold?	*He was the tallest man ever known*
10	How many degrees does a clock's hour hand pass through between 1 a.m. and 6 a.m.?	*150 degrees*
11	Which waves are shorter – television or radio waves?	*Television*
12	Which field of science has organic and inorganic branches?	*Chemistry*
13	What sort of shape is a torus?	*Like a ring doughnut*
14	What is insomnia?	*Difficulty in falling, or staying asleep*
15	What is 30 percent of 30 kilograms?	*9 kilograms*

Quiz 146
Question 8

Quiz 146
Question 9

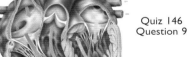

Quiz 146 Level 4

Questions

Answers

		Questions	Answers
1		What was Telstar, which came into the news in 1962?	*The first television satellite*
2		A reading of 120 over 80 is normal for an adult being tested for what?	*Blood pressure*
3		Write 543,122 to the nearest 10,000.	*540,000*
4		An alkali is the chemical opposite of what?	*An acid*
5		Lemurs are found in only one country. What is it?	*Madagascar*
6		Who would use an endoscope?	*A surgeon*
7		What are the only birds that moult their beaks?	*Puffins*
8		The designer Alec Issigonis is remembered for having designed which popular car?	*The Mini*
9		Coronary disease affects which part of the body?	*The heart*
10		What do we call the flow of electrons from one atom to another?	*The electric current*
11		Humber, Verrazano Narrows and Severn are examples of what?	*Bridge*
12		What is three million divided by six?	*500,000*
13		What sort of person would use a gyrocompass?	*An aircraft or ship pilot*
14		Which element has the lowest boiling point?	*Helium*
15		A rock called bauxite is the main source of which metal?	*Aluminium*

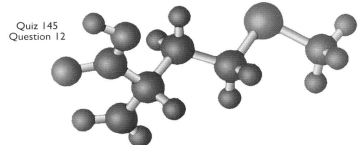

Quiz 145
Question 12

Quiz 145
Question 11

Quiz 147 Level 4

Questions

Answers

		Questions	Answers
1		What is the smallest unit of a computer's visual display?	*A pixel*
2		What are all the letters used in Roman numerals?	*M, D, C, L, X, V, I*
3		Dry ice is frozen what?	*Carbon dioxide*
4		What is a sudden rise in water level, caused by the tide pushing up a narrow passage, called?	*A tidal bore*
5		Glaucoma affects which part of the body?	*The eyes*
6		What does an entomologist study?	*Insects*
7		Polythene is a type of what?	*Plastic*
8		The Bering Strait separates which two continents?	*Asia and North America*
9		If the perimeter of a rectangle is six times its 6 cm width, what is its length?	*12 cm*
10		What is a scientist who studies the characteristics of human beings called?	*Anthropologist*
11		What does equilibrium mean?	*In a state of balance*
12		What develops inside a woman's ovary?	*A human egg*
13		What type of farming uses 'steps' on a hillside to prevent water from running off the fields?	*Terrace farming*
14		What type of animal is a Portuguese Man of War?	*Jellyfish*
15		Write 4,781 to the nearest hundred.	*4,800*

Quiz 148
Question 3

Quiz 148
Question 4

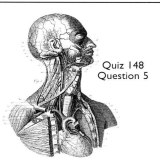

Quiz 148
Question 5

Quiz 148 Level 4

Questions

Answers

		Question	Answer
1		Which was the first city to have an underground railway system?	*London*
2		What does 'pneumatic' mean?	*Filled with, or powered by, air*
3		Using a single die, what are the chances of throwing a two?	*⅙*
4		What three letters were used to mean a video recorder?	*VCR*
5		What is the study of the structure of the human body?	*Anatomy*
6		What type of animal is a herbivore?	*One that eats only plants*
7		Doctors prescribe quinine in order to treat which disease?	*Malaria*
8		On which continent would you find the Great Rift Valley?	*Africa*
9		How many centimetres are there in a kilometre?	*100,000*
10		What type of safety device melts if too much electricity passes through it?	*A fuse*
11		What does it mean if an animal is described as being feral?	*It has reverted to its behaviour in the wild*
12		What part of the body does a podiatrist treat?	*The feet*
13		What process causes a teaspoon to become hot if left in a cup of tea?	*Conduction*
14		What is animal husbandry?	*Managing animals for food production*
15		What types of food would someone on a vegan diet avoid?	*Meats, fish and all dairy products*

Quiz 147
Question 6

Quiz 147
Question 14

Quiz 149 Level 4

	Questions	Answers
1	A truck carries 1,500 kg. How many loads will it take to move 30,000 kg?	20
2	What is measured in decibels?	Sound
3	If a scientist comes up with a figure in amperes, what is he or she measuring?	Electric current
4	What is the condition called when someone has lost so much body heat they are in physical danger?	Hypothermia
5	A dynamo is a type of what device?	Generator
6	What does it mean if a material is synthetic?	It is made by people and is not natural
7	An orthopaedic surgeon specializes in treating which part of the body?	Bones
8	What are tweeters and subwoofers types of?	Speaker
9	Which is the deepest lake in the world?	Lake Baikal
10	What is the 50 multiplied by 0.5?	25
11	What does 'translucent' mean?	Allowing light to shine through
12	What does 'R&D' stand for?	Research and Development
13	What is the cocoon stage in the life of an animal such as a butterfly called?	A pupa
14	According to most scientists, which catastrophic event caused the dinosaurs to die away?	An asteroid hit the Earth
15	What percentage of an hour is 45 minutes?	75 percent

Quiz 150
Question 14

Quiz 150
Question 12

Quiz 150 Level 4

	Questions	Answers
1	What type of animal is an omnivore?	*One that eats both plants and animals*
2	What links the structure of the planets Jupiter, Saturn, Uranus and Neptune?	*They are giant balls of gas*
3	Water leaks from a tap at a rate of 200 ml every five minutes. How much will leak in five hours?	*12 litres*
4	What does DTP stand for?	*Desk-top publishing*
5	Clarence Birdseye is known as the founder of which industry?	*Frozen food*
6	What part of the body does the disease emphysema affect?	*The lungs*
7	How would you appear if you looked at yourself in a concave mirror?	*Upside down*
8	The word 'Jovian' describes which aspect of our Solar System?	*The planet Jupiter*
9	What is the science that studies human characteristics and how they are passed on?	*Genetics*
10	Write 615,334 to the nearest 100.	*615,300*
11	What is a meteor that lands on Earth called?	*A meteorite*
12	What is the 'eider' of an eiderdown?	*Duck feathers*
13	What is a metal beam used in constructing skyscrapers and other large buildings called?	*A girder*
14	Penny bun, chanterelle and shitake are all types of what?	*Mushroom*
15	A car travels at 60 km/h. How far will it travel between 0900 and 1330?	*270 km*

Quiz 149
Question 8

Quiz 149
Question 13

Quiz 151 Level 4

	Questions	Answers
1	What is a stoat called when it has white fur?	*Ermine*
2	What is hypertension?	*Constant high blood pressure*
3	How many days are there in 14 weeks, six days?	*104 days*
4	Which constellation is sometimes called the Lion?	*Leo*
5	How many digits are there in the binary system?	*Two*
6	What is a cygnet?	*A young swan*
7	What type of animal builds a lodge?	*Beaver*
8	What is another word for a video camera used for making home movies?	*Camcorder*
9	Which part of the body has a root, a pulp cavity and dentine?	*The teeth*
10	What is the name of the large fault that threatens San Francisco and other parts of California?	*The San Andreas Fault*
11	How many days will four and a half tonnes of potatoes last if 125 kg are used each day?	*36 days*
12	What is the chemical symbol for potassium?	*K*
13	What does a chiropractor do?	*Adjusts people's spines to relieve pain*
14	On which continent is Patagonia?	*South America*
15	Which two tasks does a combine harvester actually combine?	*Cutting the crop and beating the grain*

Quiz 152
Question 11

Quiz 152
Question 3

Quiz 152
Question 15